Science under Siege?

Interest Groups and the Science Wars

Leon E. Trachtman and Robert Perrucci

ROWMAN & LITTLEFIELD PUBLISHERS, INC.
Lanham • Boulder • New York • Oxford

ROWMAN & LITTLEFIELD PUBLISHERS, INC.

Published in the United States of America
by Rowman & Littlefield Publishers, Inc.
4720 Boston Way, Lanham, Maryland 20706
www.rowmanlittlefield.com

12 Hid's Copse Road
Cumnor Hill, Oxford OX2 9JJ, England

British Library Cataloguing in Publication Information Available

Library of Congress Cataloging-in-Publication Data

Trachtman, Leon E., 1925–
    Science under siege? : interest groups and the science wars / Leon E. Trachtman
and Robert Perrucci.
        p. cm.
    Includes bibliographical references and index.
    ISBN 0-8476-9800-9 (alk. paper)—ISBN 0-8476-9801-7 (pbk. : alk. paper)
    1. Science—Social aspects. 2. Science and state. I. Perrucci, Robert.
II. Title.
Q175.55.T73 2000
303.48'3—dc21   00-029085

Printed in the United States of America

♾ ™ The paper used in this publication meets the minimum requirements of
American National Standard for Information Sciences—Permanence of Paper
for Printed Library Materials, ANSI Z39.48–1992.

Contents

Preface

The origins of this book lie in the classroom. In 1996 the authors were co-instructors of a course offered jointly in Purdue University's departments of communication and sociology and anthropology. We planned and taught the course because we shared two interests, one substantive and the other methodological. Our substantive interest was the so-called science wars: the alleged attack on science by a variety of critics led by the post-modern social constructivists of the "academic left" and including assorted groups of environmentalists, feminists, and scientific creationists. Methodologically, we were interested in exploring and in teaching our students (and ourselves) a variety of approaches to conducting highly qualitative and in-depth interviews and interview analysis. The class was organized democratically, and its structure was the product of many intense and free-ranging discussions of our interests, expectations, and goals.

We first surveyed the literature of both the presumed attackers and defenders of science. This led us to pose a number of questions. Was the "war" being waged on broad or narrow grounds? Did it consist of philosophical and epistemological discourse at a highly rarefied level or did it concern itself with the practical problems of a runaway science-technology? Were the opinions and arguments those of a small and insular national elite or of large groups of critics at the grass roots? Did the criticisms expressed reflect a broad and unified social vision or a variety of narrow parochial interests?

As we discussed these and related questions, the form of our inquiry began to emerge. We would develop appropriate interview instruments, pretest them on several subjects, modify them as needed, and administer them to six selected groups of respondents. The problems of designing the interview protocols and developing methods of coding and analysis provided the students with practical experience in coping with the difficulties of organizing bodies of relatively unstructured interview materials.

Our students were enthusiastic participants in the work of the course. Indeed, when it became apparent that we would not come close to completing the project during a single semester, almost all of them eagerly agreed to sign up for a second semester's continuation of the class to enable them to see the work through to completion. During this second semester we were able to finish most of the work of interviewing and analysis. Several students were able to stay in touch with the project even after the end of this semester and to make a number of helpful suggestions as we began to organize our materials for publication.

Some of the conclusions of the study have been made available in other forums. Along with student Michael Dennis, we presented some of our findings at the thirteenth National Science, Technology and Society Conference in Chicago, on May 5, 1998, and we published an abbreviated version of the project in the *International Journal of Contemporary Sociology*, volume 35, number 2, October 1998.

The present volume provides a far fuller and richer conceptual and historical context for our project and explores in much greater depth some of the possible implications of the science wars for both science and society.

The order of our names on this book does not reflect any distinction in responsibility or workload. We simply follow the practice of alternating the order of authorship across publications.

We would like to acknowledge the contributions and the invaluable assistance of the following students, without whom the project could not have been accomplished: Greg Carender, Changfu Chang, Constance Chay, Shiv Ganesh, Matt Hoevel, Nate Letsinger, Abby Lyon, Jennifer McKinney, Linda Orr, Michael Schlehuber, and Jennifer Wille. Special mention must be made of Michael Dennis, who contributed above and beyond expectations to one of the chapters. Thanks, too, to Harry Epstein, who made very helpful comments on one of the early treatments of the material. We learned at least as much from this band of bright and eager students as we were able to teach them.

We are especially indebted to Dean Birkenkamp for his strong support of this project, and to others at Rowman & Littlefield who helped to bring the project to completion: Ann Abel, Matt Boullioun, and Karen Johnson.

In addition, heartfelt thanks to Candy Lawson for preparation of the final manuscript and Carolyn Parrish for transcribing taped interviews.

Chapter 1

Science under Siege:
Historical Perspective

If we were to identify a specific year in which science and science-based technology were held in the highest esteem by the general public, it might well be 1960. Fifteen years earlier, victory in World War II had been achieved with the invaluable assistance of the U.S. and British scientific and technological establishments, which had produced a war-ending atomic weapon, radar, cybernetic controls of anti-aircraft fire, noise filters for radio and telephonic communication, and other militarily useful technologies. The combined scientific and technological achievements of both the Allied and the Axis nations, including such developments as jet engines, rocketry, and missile guidance systems, demonstrated to political leaders and the general public alike the indispensability of scientists and technologists to a modern nation's military security.

In the decade following the war, spokesmen for the scientific establishment played an increasingly active and decisive role in shaping the nation's policies toward science and technology and setting national research priorities. Wandering the halls of Congress and testifying before congressional committees, scientific leaders were instrumental in the creation and expansion of government agencies charged with a variety of scientific and technological missions: the Atomic Energy Commission; the National Science Foundation; a greatly expanded National Institutes of Health; the National Aeronautics and Space Administration; such units within the Department of Defense as the Office of Naval Research, the Army Research Office, and the Air Force Office of Scientific Research; and later, the Department of Energy. Political leaders accepted the greatly expanded role of the federal government in the conduct of scientific research and development, partly out of the conviction that it was a necessity for national defense in an increasingly menacing Cold War and partly to repay the U.S. scientific establishment for

1

redirecting many of its activities toward military objectives in the recently concluded war.

On October 4, 1957, the Soviet satellite Sputnik was sent into orbit, becoming the first successful entry of a human artifact into space. By 1960 the idea of space travel as a supreme achievement of human technology had captured the imagination of the public in many nations, so much so that achievements in this area were used as symbolic counters in the bloodless conflict between the West and the Soviet bloc. To this end, the U.S. public was swept up in the youthful John F. Kennedy's 1960 vow to put a man—a U.S. man—on the moon within the decade.

During these heady times for science, annual appropriations for the conduct of research and development increased at a rate unmatched either before or since. "Research" was the magic word, and it was expected to solve all our problems, from providing a supply of safe, inexpensive, and virtually inexhaustible energy to developing cures for mental and emotional illness. And indeed, our research efforts did yield a variety of striking achievements in such fields as biomedicine, space science, and information and communication technology. So attractive was this palmy time for science that Dixy Lee Ray, a former Atomic Energy Commissioner, gushed over it retrospectively in 1990 as follows:

> [It] was a time when experts were believed. It was also a time of unprecedented increase in our knowledge about the world, of belief in ourselves, and in our ability through understanding and logic to provide adequate solutions to technical problems.
>
> It was a time of improvement in the conditions of living that made our society and our nation the envy of the world. It was a time when the use of knowledge was expected, when the myriad applications of science through technology made living on the earth easier and better.[1]

While there is undoubtedly truth in Ray's assessment of the spirit and achievement of the early 1960s, it is also a narrow and rather naïve appraisal of how things were and why they seemed to have deteriorated so markedly since then (she blames an ignorant and sensation-oriented press for misinforming and frightening an uninformed and impressionable public). Still, Ray was correct in asserting that since that time, many observers have intuitively sensed a decline in and erosion of public confidence in science and technology. This sort of phenomenon is, of course, extremely difficult to quantify. In addition, one is hard pressed to decide whether such a decline and erosion have taken place across a broad segment of the population or whether they represent only the attitudes of a small number of self-appointed and highly visible and audible critics.

It is the appearance of these critiques from a number of quarters and the response to them from some members of the scientific community that have, in recent years, come to be known as the science wars. We propose, in this book, to try to provide an understanding of the science wars that goes beyond reiterating the militant and defensive statements of a small number of the most visible combatants.

CRITICISM OF SCIENCE AND TECHNOLOGY

Of course, as far back as we can identify human activities as "scientific" or "technological," our mythologies have warned against the hubris that so often accompanies our efforts and achievements in these areas. Both historically and mythologically, technological man and man seeking scientific understanding of the natural world have often been described as attempting to transcend the limitations placed upon them by God or gods and aspiring to reach a forbidden God-like state of knowledge. A number of examples of this attitude have been cited so often as to have become clichés:

- The builders of the technologically marvelous Tower of Babel, perceived by God as trying, by technological means, to reach a precinct forbidden to them, were frustrated in their attempts by God's imposing on them a multitude of mutually unintelligible languages.
- Prometheus, the titan who tried to enhance human technological abilities by providing man with the gift of fire from heaven, suffered eternal punishment at the hands of Zeus for thus contributing to the growth of human pride and arrogance.
- Dr. Faustus, a medieval alchemist, willingly sold his soul to the devil in exchange for the power he would gain from having unlimited knowledge.
- Mary Shelley's Dr. Frankenstein was destroyed by the product of his technological triumph.

Similarly, modern science, since its beginnings in the middle of the seventeenth century, has never been immune to criticism despite its remarkable record of success in illuminating the natural world and helping to prompt technological advances over a wide front. As early as 1726 Jonathan Swift published a biting parody of the work of the British Royal Society in the third book of *Gulliver's Travels*. Captain Lemuel Gulliver, set adrift by pirates during the course of his third journey, makes his way to the kingdom of Laputa, a nation of speculative thinkers "so wrapped up in cogitation that [they are] in manifest danger of falling down every precipice, and bouncing [their heads] against every post." This nation of impractical astronomers and geometers is exceeded in folly only by the inhabitants of the neighboring nation of Balnibarbi, of which Gulliver says, "I never knew a soil so unhappily cultivated, houses so ill-contrived and so ruinously, or a people whose countenances and habit expressed so much misery and want." About forty years before Gulliver's arrival, following a visit to Laputa, a group of Balnibarbians fell into schemes "of putting all arts, sciences, languages and mechanics upon a new foot." To accomplish this they created an academy of projectors in Lagado their capital city, and counterparts in every other town of the kingdom.

> In these colleges, the professors contrived new rules and methods of agriculture and building, and new instruments and tools for all trades and manufactures, whereby, as they undertake, one man shall do the work of ten, a palace may be built in a week, of materials so durable as to last forever without repairing. All the fruits of the earth shall come to maturity at whatever season we think fit to choose, and increase an hundredfold more than they do at present, with innumerable other happy proposals. The only inconvenience is, that none of these projects are yet brought to perfection, and in the meantime the whole country lies miserably waste, the houses in ruins, and the people without food or clothes.[2]

Undeterred, however, by their lack of success in making practical applications of their harebrained theoretical schemes, the Balnibarbians, "driven equally on by hope and despair," prosecute their projects with fifty times the commitment and violence. To see some of the projectors at work, Gulliver is escorted to the Grand Academy of Lagado—a caricature of the British Royal Society. The first projector he sees is a man "with sooty hands and face, his hair and beard long, ragged and singed in several places." He has been working for eight years on a project for extracting sunbeams out of cucumbers, "which were to be put into vials hermetically sealed, and let out to warm the air in raw inclement summers." He told Gulliver that he did not doubt that he would achieve success in eight more years, and by that time should be able to supply the Governor's gardens with sunshine at a reasonable rate. Since his stock was low, this projector begged a gift of money from Gulliver "as an encouragement to ingenuity."

A second projector, more filthy than the first, was attempting to reduce human excrement to its original food by "separating the several parts, removing the tincture which it receives from the gall, making the odour exhale and scumming off the saliva."

Among the other projectors were an architect "who had contrived a new method of building houses, by beginning at the roof and working downwards to the foundation," and a man born blind, with several comparably blind assistants, who was attempting to mix colors for painters by feel and smell. Unfortunately, like all the other projectors at the academy, they had as yet met with no success in making practical application of their theoretical speculations. From Swift's time until the present, science has never been free of criticism that characterized its practitioners as foolish, muddleheaded, absentminded, and impractical, and its methods as cold, unfeeling, and inhumane. During the age of Romanticism, for example, doubts about the goals and methods of science were expressed by a variety of European and American thinkers. From Johann Wolfgang von Goethe (despite his standing as an amateur experimental scientist) to the English poet and mystic William Blake, a broad spectrum of artists and philosophers expressed skepticism about science as an approach to understanding the true essence of reality.

In 1842 a book worthy of the dreamiest of the Balnibarbian projectors was published in the United States. It was called *The Paradise Within the Reach of All Men, Without Labor, by Powers of Nature and Machinery: An Address to All Intelligent Men.* Its author was John Adolphous Etzler, a visionary German immigrant. In this volume, Etzler joined the company of nineteenth-century technological enthusiasts who believed that no scientific-technological accomplishment was beyond the capability of their ingenuity and their machinery. In *The Paradise*, Etzler exclaimed:

> Fellow-men! I promise to show the means of creating a paradise within ten years, where everything desirable for human life may be had by every man in super-abundance, without labor, and without pay; where the whole face of nature shall be changed into the most beautiful forms, and man may live in the most magnificent palaces, in all imaginable refinements of luxury, and in the most delightful gardens; where he may accomplish without labor, in one year, more than hitherto could be done in thousands of years; may level mountains, sink valleys, create lakes, may explore the interior of the globe, provide himself with the means, unheard of yet, for increasing his knowledge of the world, and so his intelligence; lead a life of continual happiness, of enjoyments yet unknown; [and] free himself from almost all the evils that affect mankind, except death.[3]

As it happens, the reviewer of Etzler's book in the November 1843 *Democratic Review* was one Henry David Thoreau, an expert pencil-maker, poet, essayist, philosopher, and technological skeptic of Concord, Massachusetts. Lumping Etzler with the other technological experts of the day, Thoreau parodied their naïve expectations and assurances about the possibilities and the consequences of technology:

> Let us not succumb to nature. We will marshal the clouds and restrain tempests; we will bottle up pestilent exhalations; we will probe for earthquakes, grub them up, and give vent to the dangerous gas; we will disembowel the volcano, and extract its poison, take its seed out. We will wash water, and warm

fire, and cool ice, and underprop the earth. We will teach birds to fly, and fishes to swim, and ruminants to chew the cud. It is time we looked into these things.[4]

After thus mocking the hubris of these nineteenth-century counterparts of the projectors of Lagado's Grand Academy in making extravagant and absurd claims for their technologies, Thoreau pillories science and technology for their "superficial and violent" treatment of nature. As an astute student of science and a skilled technologist, he understood the physical fallacies of Etzler's ambitions and claims and pointed them out pithily. But of even more concern to Thoreau than the physical impossibility of Etzler's schemes was the offensive "baseness and grossness" of a vision for the future that defined human aspirations in such purely material terms. It is in this regard that Thoreau exemplifies the Romantic concern for the spiritual, the moral, and the intuitive and its indifference to a science and technology that "aim to secure the greatest degree of gross comfort and pleasure merely."

In like fashion, Walt Whitman shared the Romantic emphasis on feeling over reason and spirituality over rationality as means of understanding the truest essence of reality. This perspective on life is perhaps best illustrated in his "When I Heard the Learn'd Astronomer."

> When I heard the learn'd astronomer,
> When the proofs, the figures, were ranged in columns before me,
> When I was shown the charts and diagrams, to add, divide, and measure them,
> When I sitting heard the astronomer where he lectured with much applause in the lecture-room,
> How soon unaccountable I became tired and sick,
> Till rising and gliding out I wander'd off by myself
> In the mystical moist night-air, and from time to time,
> Look'd up in perfect silence at the stars.[5]

RELATIONS OF SCIENCE AND TECHNOLOGY

But despite this undertone in recent Western culture of questioning and criticizing science, science has consistently been among the most highly respected and esteemed professions. It is essential, at this point, to clarify the relationship between science and technology. At the beginning of science's modern era some three hundred years ago, the gulf between science and technology was almost as great as it had been for the preceding two or three millennia. The roots of science in the ancient world lay very close to the disciplines of philosophy and religion. As construed in classical Greece, science was a speculative and explanatory pursuit having little or nothing in common with technology, which was a practical and utilitarian art grounded in the activities of essentially atheoretical artisans. Indeed, those cultures of the past that emphasized and practiced science as natural philosophy tended to lag somewhat in the development of practical and useful technologies, while those that produced triumphs of applied technology tended to slight or even ignore the theoretical musings of science. It was only in the nineteenth century that science and technology became more securely wedded to each other, largely on account of their increasing mutual dependence. But even then there were social and caste differences, as the elitist professors in the recently developed German scientific universities looked at technology as both subsequent and subordinate to basic, or "pure," science. At the same time, practical inventors tended to view theoretically grounded science as somewhat airy and irrelevant to their goal of improving the quality of life through the design and manufacture of useful machines and devices. But even in these early years of modern science the occasional individual was able to bridge the gulf traditionally separating the practitioners of science and technology. Benjamin Franklin is perhaps the most prominent example of these early scientist-inventors.

As the number of scientists and the volume of research increased during the course of the nineteenth and early twentieth centuries, the interdependence of science and technology became ever more apparent. Technological development became less serendipitous and less the product of trial and error iterations, and far more scientized, needing and flowing from the rapidly expanding body of confirmed, organized, and cataloged information about the physical world provided by science, while the progress of science became ever more dependent on technology to provide the tools, techniques, and instruments required for basic research. This closer wedding of science and technology is largely the reason that contemporary programs of philosophical, historical, sociological, anthropological, and political scholarship about these aspects of our culture are almost universally called STS, standing for either Science and Technology Studies or Science, Technology, and Society.

While it is still possible to make theoretical and practical distinctions between science and technology, the differences between the two become ever less significant, especially in such fields as solid-state physics and biotechnology. John Ziman, for example, points out that, in studying the phenomenon of fatigue in metals, "we are almost forced into the position of saying that on Monday, Wednesday and Friday we are just honest seekers after truth whilst on Tuesday, Thursday and Saturday we are practical chaps trying to stop aeroplanes from falling to pieces."[6]

Indeed, it is extremely common for respondents in man-in-the-street opinion samples, when asked how science has benefited them, to list jet planes, television, computers, and open-heart surgery as the "scientific" advances that have most improved the quality of their lives. And to be honest, one

can probably make the case that there is enough "science" in all these technologies to justify this opinion.

As we have noted, general esteem for this relatively new hybrid—science-
technology—seems to have peaked in around 1960, when such war-born
and other contributions as nuclear power and antibiotics seemed poised to
make Etzler's predictions of a century earlier into reality. What has happened in the past almost forty years to erode this esteem? It appears that a
variety of political events, social movements, and academic inquiries have
conspired to raise questions about science's favored place and, perhaps, to
undermine its privileged position in public opinion. Sorting out the sources
and impacts of these events and movements and characterizing their interre-
lationships is difficult; some seem to have appeared simultaneously with
others by mere chance while others may well be related consequences of the
same basic cause. And deciding which are causes and which are effects can
be similarly problematical.

One major category of these critiques of science seems to be largely theoretical and epistemological, dealing with the nature of scientific knowledge,
its origins, methods, and limitations, while another category is primarily political and social, concerned with the attitudes, motives, and behavior of scientists and the practical and societal consequences of their work. There are,
of course, major areas of overlap between these two classes of critique.

EPISTEMOLOGICAL CRITIQUES OF SCIENCE

In 1962 Thomas Kuhn first published his now ubiquitous study, *The Structure of Scientific Revolutions.*[7] In his analysis of the growth and development of scientific knowledge, Kuhn questioned some of the assumptions of
both positivistic theory and traditional history of science that viewed its
growth as steady, accretive, and cumulative. Traditional positivism of the
nineteenth century proposed that all true knowledge can be established by
experiment in accordance with established laws of science and can be veri-
fied by the evidence of the senses. Logical positivism is the variety of traditional positivism produced by the Vienna Circle in the first half of the twentieth century, which attempted to develop logical and linguistic systems that
would express lines of reasoning in all the sciences. Members of the Vienna
Circle hoped the mathematical theory of logical systems so developed would
produce unambiguous and totally consensible proofs in all of science.

Kuhn attempted to refute positivistic thought by demonstrating that the
same data and evidence can and do mean different things to observers in
different times and places and operating in the context of different paradigms or theoretical and conceptual models. Given this epistemological assumption, Kuhn asserts that it is no longer possible to accept the traditional

view of scientific growth and development as a pure process of accretion. Rather, successive generations of scientists appear to bring to the interpretation of data different conceptual frameworks that confer different meanings on the data. Careful study of the history of the physical sciences, then, reveals what really happened at the major turning points associated with such names as Copernicus, Newton, Lavoisier, and Einstein. Rather than contributing new, illuminating, and previously unknown data, their work precipitated conceptual revolutions that "necessitated the community's rejection of one time-honored scientific theory in favor of another incompatible with it. Each produced a consequent shift in the problems available for scientific scrutiny and in the standards by which the profession determined what should count as an admissable problem or as a legitimate problem-solution."[8] This insight led to the widespread use of the term "paradigm shift" to apply to everything from relativity theory to child-rearing practices.

Whatever the merits or demerits of Kuhn's fundamental concept and its popular interpretations and applications, the effect on social studies of science was profound and far-reaching. By suggesting the fallacy of viewing scientific knowledge as absolute, objective, and universal, Kuhn opened the door to a new epistemological understanding of science that had the potential to undermine its privileged status. A few years after the publication and widespread acceptance of Kuhn's work, a group of sociologists and historians at the University of Edinburgh began to produce analyses of historical science that launched the idea that scientific knowledge, rather than being fixed and stable for all of its producers and consumers, was "socially constructed." In the introduction to *Natural Order*, a collection of such analyses, editors Barry Barnes and Steven Shapin write:

> Perhaps the most significant change in the history of science, and indeed in the study of science generally, over the last decade is that it has become more relaxed and naturalistic. Increasingly, we have become prepared to treat science as an aspect of our culture like any other. The intense concern of earlier generations with the special status of science and its allegedly distinctive characteristics has begun to ebb away. Without any great proclamation or catastrophic upheaval in method, scholars have been increasingly willing to accept accounts of scientific change simply as the techniques of their discipline reveal it to them, and to perceive less and less need for a "rational reconstruction" of the past. There is now a real interest in our natural knowledge as a product of our way of life, as something we have constructed rather than something which has been, so to speak, revealed to us.
>
> If this tendency continues, if we relax completely about natural knowledge and set it alongside technique, art, music or literature as simply a part of our culture, then some interesting consequences will follow.[9]

Barnes and Shapin go on to "reject the spurious distinction between the internal intellectual history of the rational growth of knowledge, and the external social history, dealing with alleged irrational influences upon it." Asserting that "science stands symmetrically with other forms of culture," these proponents of the so-called "strong programme" began to develop a literature about science "explicitly concerned with natural knowledge as culture, and explicitly exploring the possibilities of anthropological and sociological methods in understanding it." Although the editors of this initial collection of essays did not impose any special unifying scheme on the articles included, they did solicit contributions with "a naturalistic approach."

Around the time these and other social scientists, primarily in Great Britain, western Europe and the United States, were exploring the possibilities of treating the history of science as an aspect of culture rather than as a rational retrospective reconstruction of what actually happened, the allure of modernism as a philosophical and esthetic model began to dim. Although the modernism that had dominated much artistic and social thought for the first half of the twentieth century had two faces—one orderly, rational, and optimistic and the other, manifested more in the arts than in philosophy, irrational and alienated—the chief social and philosophical thrust of modernism envisions that human society may be perfected through rational management and by the development and application of technology. It is apparent that scientific positivism fits well with this social outlook.

The attitudes of modernism may best be understood by considering the theoretical basis of Frederick W. Taylor's "scientific management." Through systematic observation and analysis of workers at work, Taylor developed highly organized and rational models of performance that attempted to eliminate wasted motion and general inefficiency. The technocratic spirit of scientific management, applied by William Leffingwell in the office as well as on the factory floor, and prescribed for more efficient management of farms, businesses, churches, colleges and universities, government, and the home, represents the utopian spirit of modernism that transcends particular models of social organization, since it appealed equally to managers in the capitalist United States and in the communist Soviet Union.

By the middle of the century, it was apparent that modernism had failed to produce a perfect, rational, planned, and compassionate world. This realization undermined the belief that society could be perfected through centralized planning and technological development. The chaotic and sometimes violent spirit of the late 1960s and early 1970s gave rise to postmodern thought, an irrational, ironic, and self-referential approach to society and its illusions about the efficacy of planned, rational, and technocratic action. Disillusionment with orderly and rational planning of society naturally had a spin-off effect of raising doubts about the goals and methods of science, by definition the most logically planned and rationally executed of human activities.

At the same time, academic life witnessed the emergence of the deconstructionist school of literary criticism, most closely associated with the French scholar and critic Jacques Derrida. This theory of criticism asserts that there is no single meaning that can be extracted from a text. The reader of the text becomes co-equal with the author as a creator of meanings and, through a variety of interpretations, the text can be shown to have multiple meanings. This variety of meanings can be related to social status and political power and alliances of both creators and interpreters of texts. If this is true, then claims to universality in art disappear, and the complex relationships between author, reader, and text reveal unanticipated and unintended nuances and meanings extractable from the text under different circumstances. This approach almost always has as one of its effects the disempowering of the author and the vitiation of his or her intentions.

It is but a short step, in the context of Kuhnian analysis of this history of science, to apply these same deconstructionist techniques of analysis to works of science. As displayed in the work of Bruno Latour and Steve Woolgar, among others, scientific "truths" are posited as socially constructed rather than as universal for all times, places, and observers. Application of different paradigms, or conceptual frames of reference, to bodies of scientific data yields different conclusions.

Harry Collins and Trevor Pinch, in *The Golem: What Everyone Should Know about Science*, attempt to depict science not as a privileged domain of knowledge in which universal consensus is possible, but rather as an intensely human activity. Although their depictions and analyses of a number of unresolved—and perhaps unresolvable—scientific projects lead them to a conclusion neither pro- nor anti-science, their interpretation of science as a socially constructed activity leads to new ways of understanding science. They write:

> As things . . . stand we have only two ways of thinking about science; it is all good or all bad. Unstable Equilibrium—flip-flop thinking—is the inevitable consequence of a model of science and technology which is supposed to deliver complete certainty. The trouble is that both states of the flip-flop are to be feared. The overweening claims to authority of many scientists and technologists are offensive and unjustified but the likely reaction, born of failed promises, might precipitate *a still worse anti-scientific movement*. Scientists should promise less; they might then be better able to keep their promises.[10] [italics added]

Although Collins and Pinch, like many students of science and technology as social phenomena, take a neutral stance between excessive scientism and anti-scientism, their analysis is viewed by many scientists as undermining the legitimate authority of expertise and therefore as firing an offensive salvo in the science wars. Collins and Pinch, on the other hand, like most social constructionists, believe that the general public would be better served if accounts of science and technology took into consideration the false starts and missteps, the political and social influences, and the wide range of inferences and interpretations possible from the same data, and ceased their retrospective transmutation of the often ambiguous realities of scientific and technological efforts into "neat and tidy scientific myth(s)." If scientific "truths" were more widely viewed as "constructed" and therefore conditional and provisional rather than as the thoroughly objective and universal products of disembodied and totally disinterested scientific minds, there would be far less public disillusionment when these "truths" prove to be not necessarily true.

MERTON'S NORMS OF SCIENCE

The claims of universality, objectivity, and disinterestedness on the part of scientists, while dating back in some fashion to the early years of modern science, were first codified as a social model of scientific behavior in the 1930s and 1940s by Robert Merton, probably the pre-eminent sociologist of science in the twentieth century. Originally published under the title "Science and Technology in a Democratic Order" in 1952, Merton's landmark essay was reprinted in his 1973 book, *Social Research and the Practicing Professions*, under the title "The Normative Structure of Science."[11] In this essay, Merton characterizes the ethos of science as "that affectively toned complex of values and norms which is held to be binding on scientists." These norms are expressed "in the form of prescriptions, preferences, permissions and proscriptions" and are "legitimized in terms of institutional values." To the end of furthering the institutional goal of science, which Merton takes to be "the extension of certified knowledge," he identifies four institutional imperatives that compose the ethos of modern science: universalism, communism, disinterestedness, and organized skepticism.

The norm of universalism is grounded in the impersonality of the pre-established criteria against which the truth-claims of science must be subjected. These criteria must be "consonant with observation and previously confirmed knowledge." As a consequence, acceptance or rejection of scientific truth-claims must be independent of personal or social attributes of their protagonists: race, nationality, religion, gender, social class, and other irrelevant characteristics. These claims, grounded in impersonality, must necessarily be objective, and "objectivity precludes particularism." Certified scientific knowledge, therefore, being independent of particular personal characteristics of its proponent or its venue, must in principle appear the same to all observers. While Merton concedes that the principle of universalism may be put into practice inadequately, it remains as science's dominant guiding tenet.

The second of Merton's norms is communism, construed in this context as common ownership of the intellectual goods that science comprises. Scientific knowledge "constitutes a common heritage in which the equity of the individual producer is severely limited," since "the substantive findings of science are a product of social collaboration and are assigned to the community." Although he grants the universal concern of scientists with establishing priority, this competitiveness for recognition "does not challenge the status of scientific knowledge as common property." In fulfillment of the standard of communism, Merton asserts that "secrecy is the antithesis of this norm and open communication its enactment."

The third norm is disinterestedness—the absence of commitments or interests on the part of scientists that will influence their observations or interpretations of scientific research. Merton rejects the notion that disinterestedness can be equated with altruism or that interested action identifies with egotism. Rather, what he describes as "the virtual absence of fraud in the annals of science" stems not from any unusual degree of moral integrity on the part of those who choose to embark on scientific careers, but rather from the structure and methods of the scientific community that enforce rigorous policing procedures to test the reproducibility and verifiability of the results. It is "the exacting scrutiny of fellow experts," rooted in the public and testable character of science, that forces both the acceptance and the practical application of the norm of disinterestedness.

This leads very naturally to Merton's fourth norm: organized skepticism. The whole structure of science, with its peer review procedures and insistence on replicability of experiment, makes every scientist into a critic as well as a producer, disseminator, and consumer of scientific information. The process of science works if, and only if, each scientist brings to the examination of others' research results an analytical and tough-minded skepticism and a refusal to accept on faith and without adequate scrutiny the results reported by scientific colleagues.

Merton's four norms compose an interacting and mutually reinforcing system of behavior designed to make the common intellectual property of science proof against the distorting possibilities that arise if shared scientific knowledge is not treated as the universal and impersonal product of disinterested scientists and as fair game for criticism by a variety of juries of peers. If all scientists take seriously their roles as producers, distributors, consumers, and critics of scientific information and adopt the habits of mind and the behaviors prescribed by Merton's four norms, the whole process of science will truly be directed to the gathering and codifying of knowledge about the natural world in the most effective and least distorting way ever devised.

Until the early 1960s there existed a ruling assumption that Merton's norms accurately described the way scientists actually functioned and the methods by which the natural and material world can most effectively be coaxed to yield up its secrets. In the view of many scientists and observers of science, with rare exceptions they still characterize the patterns of scientific investigation and remain the guiding professional principles of the vast majority of scientists.

But some more recent conceptions of the epistemology of science and investigations of science as a social system have suggested to many social scientists that the four norms, if they were *ever* the dominant determinants of scientists' behavior, are no longer so for many scientists. Further, the assertion is made that the social, political, economic, and cultural contexts within which scientific research is conducted necessarily make much of the resultant knowledge a paradigm-bound, provisional, and conditional cultural product, and not the universal and privileged body of theory and data that many chroniclers of science have described in their retrospective reconstructions of scientific discovery.

If science is necessarily a social product that does not and cannot consist of impersonal, objective truth-claims independent of the culture, race, nationality, religion, gender, social class, or economic interest of the scientist, the norm of universality is necessarily violated. Truth claims, assert the social constructivist analysts and critics of science, cannot help but reflect the particularism of the individuals and the institutions doing and supporting the work. Clearly, defenders of science reject this assault on their most cherished and most highly valued beliefs and insist on the necessity of the universality of truth-claims, in the absence of which science would be no more than a collection of idiosyncratic observations and conclusions.

Merton's second norm is that of communism. Scientists share their knowledge, and scientific knowledge is viewed as necessarily in the public domain. The insistence of many critics and analysts on the centrality of communication to the conduct of science reinforces this view of science as, in the words of John Ziman, "public knowledge." The history of scientific meetings, symposia, conferences, and conventions, and the centuries-old role of the scientific journal appear to underscore the importance of this Mertonian norm.

On the other hand, some observers of the social and political behavior of scientists suggest that there has taken place, if not a reversal, at least an erosion of information-sharing behavior in recent decades. Like many other historians and sociologists of science, Merton points out the competitive nature of science, with the need to establish priority an important motivating force for scientists. Yet he claims that traditionally the competition among scientists has been constrained by and is subordinate to the practical need of scientists to share information freely. Even the most competitive scientist finds that the free and open exchange of information yields more self-interested benefits than the withholding of information would. Not only does the withholder of scientific information become, in Merton's words, "the target for ambivalent responses," he or she also invites retaliative behavior on the part of colleagues who will refuse to share information in the informal domain. Merton claims that all scientists, including the most creative and gifted individuals, are humble in the face of "the realization that scientific advance involves the collaboration of past and present generations."

At the same time, changes in the structure of scientific institutions and in the role of individual scientists as we entered the era of Big Science have suggested to students of scientific behavior that Mertonian communism is a norm that is increasingly honored in its breach. The pre–World War II view of the scientist as the denizen of the ivory tower and the disinterested seeker of basic truths about nature has given way, in great part, to the conception of scientists as parts of institutional teams, engaged in neck-and-neck competition, not only to establish individual and institutional priority for their discoveries, but also to enjoy the financial rewards accruing from patent claims and commercial applications of their work. Although this shift, if real, is due at least in part to the changed and more commercially charged structure and organization of science, it is also probably the result of the drastic shrinking of the time gap between the discoveries of basic research and their commercial application. For example, while much of the basic biological research of the 1910s, 1920s, and 1930s had little direct or short-term applicability in the marketplace, in this age of biotechnology it is but a short step from the basic university laboratory to the application of university research in the biotechnology industry. Indeed, the typical biotechnology company is the creation of a university professor bent on capitalizing on his or her basic research discoveries. In the same way, theoretical solid-state physics research often finds short-term commercial applicability in the semiconductor industry. In many cases of professor-founded technology companies, the faculty members' employing university aids and abets the establishment of these small enterprises. It helps the university to keep valued faculty members if they receive at least moral support for their entry into the arena of commercial technology, and the mutual assistance available in collaboration between university and business employees produces payoffs to both parties.

COMPETITIVENESS IN SCIENCE

Given these circumstances, it is no wonder that observers of scientific behavior find increasing instances of unseemly competitiveness, including the withholding rather than sharing of information, greater commercial motivation in the choice of research problems, and the inappropriate entry of large industrial organizations into the university laboratory for collaborative research. All these instances of partnership among individual scientists, their universities, and the small or large companies with interests in the products of the university laboratory put the scientists in the position of sharing information only with linked commercial organizations and making Merton's third norm of disinterestedness a virtual impossibility.

In its most malignant form this spirit of unseemly and inappropriate competitiveness, for either professional recognition or financial gain, has manifested itself not just in secretiveness, but also in downright fraud: fabrication of research results, theft, plagiarism, and related sins. It is, of course, possible that the misconduct documented in such books as Broad and Wade's *Betrayers of the Truth* is nothing new, and that fraud has been part of modern science since its seventeenth-century beginnings.[12] But it seems that reports of scientific misconduct have been more numerous in the last twenty years or so, and there is no question that they have been more widely featured in the popular press. Such coverage could certainly be responsible for increasing public disaffection with science.

Scientists respond to these claims of increasing misconduct and malpractice by insisting that it is precisely the detection mechanisms of organized science that have ferreted out and identified the rare and unusual cases of scientific fraud, and asserting that it is rigorous peer review and replication of reported procedures, based upon full disclosure in scientific papers of experimental methods, that keep science honest. The apparent increase in misconduct, they say, is an artifact of increasing press coverage rather than a real phenomenon. As a result, many defenders of science resort to the "few rotten apples" explanation of disclosed misconduct rather than accepting the conclusion of some social studies of science that misconduct is a systemic attribute of the very structure of science. They claim that any barrel of apples is bound to contain a few rotten ones, and it is one of the glories of organized science that, as an institution, it is designed and admirably equipped to identify and root out these rare cases of deviance from the norm.

It is the practical application of Merton's fourth norm—organized skepticism—that makes the detection of fraud an ever-present reality in science. Reviewers and referees are equipped to identify questionable reports, and the failure of peers to duplicate findings through replication sounds the alarm. This was certainly the case several years ago when the scientific community tested Pons and Fleischman's report of cold fusion and found it, at best, wanting.[13]

But social critics of science respond that identification of the weakness of such claims as that of Pons and Fleischman is a relative rarity, and that the numerous attempts at replication of their work were undertaken only because of the enormous commercial potential of the discovery if it proved to be true. The vast majority of reported procedures and findings, they claim, are rarely if ever replicated, a conclusion confirmed by the findings of a number of studies that some large proportion, in some cases as much as half, of the papers published in scientific journals are never, ever, cited by anyone. If lack of citation implies lack of surveillance, there is no telling what amount of error or fraud lies buried in this accumulation of uncited scientific literature.

Recognizing that both the critics and the defenders of science have as yet inconclusive claims to the certainty of their positions, there seems little doubt that increasing press interest in the question of scientific error or misconduct may well have shaken public confidence in the last four decades. Additional doubts, questions, and reservations about the goals and methods of science appear to have surfaced during this time, roughly simultaneous with the emergence of the post-modern, deconstructionist, and social constructivist critiques. It is difficult to judge the degree to which these various criticisms of science represent independent and unrelated judgments by a variety of groups, each with its own program and agenda, or the mutually reinforcing views of nominally independent but conceptually linked organizations. Actually, three possibilities exist:

1. By sheer chance, a number of different interest groups happen to have launched their attacks on science at about the same time.
2. The shared interests of these varied groups stimulate them to support one another's criticisms and to integrate their questioning of science.
3. A number of developments in science itself—the emerging dominance of Big Science, the involvement of giant commercial organizations in basic university research programs, and science's growing emphasis on highly competitive efforts to apply and capitalize on basic research— have called forth similar responses by a variety of social groups.

Some of these criticisms seem to be rooted in attitudes as old as modern science itself; others appear to have been summoned up by issues and events unique to the science of the last forty years.

INDIFFERENCE TO RIGHTS OF RESEARCH SUBJECTS

One insistent theme of the anti-science critics is the sacrifice of humaneness in the conduct of science. The background of this attitude exists in accounts of the investigations carried out by German scientists under the leadership of individuals such as Dr. Josef Mengele during the Nazi regime with no regard for the safety, health, welfare, or even lives of subjects. Although this research undoubtedly yielded useful information on such issues as the physiology of hypothermia and the consequences of a variety of surgical techniques, critics find the experimental work morally reprehensible and therefore unacceptable in a civilized society. The point raised by critics is that ethically unacceptable research has also been done in free-world science.

Bad Blood, the account by James Jones of the U.S. Public Health Service's thirty-year study of the natural history of untreated syphilis, is perhaps the landmark account that prompted the development of this critique.[14] In a time when effective antibiotics were available, scientists employed by the U.S. government designed a study that used as subjects a large group of mostly illiterate African-American syphilitic males in rural Macon County, Alabama. In order to study the natural course of untreated syphilis, the subject population was divided into two groups, one receiving standard antibiotic therapy and the other, told they were suffering from "bad blood," given inert placebos for the whole duration of the research program. The quest for better information, according to critics, led the PHS scientists to deceive and injure an ignorant and vulnerable patient population. Accounts of this sort of research have helped give rise to what is virtually a new philosophical discipline—bioethics—that holds up to scrutiny a wide range of scientific behaviors that impact on patients, subjects, clients, or the general public. That ethically questionable research continues to be conducted is demonstrated by an April 15, 1998, *New York Times* story that describes a government-funded study in which poor black and Hispanic boys were given a drug to test them for tendencies toward violence.

The story goes on to recount the 1994–95 testing of brain chemistry of a group of thirty-four boys after the administration of fenfluramine, a compound since taken off the market because of "suspected links to heart-valve damage in adults." Critics of the research claim it offered no medical benefits and put the children at risk. One asserts that the "racist and morally offensive studies" put minority children at risk simply to prove they are generally predisposed to be violent in the future.[15]

At the same time that studies using human subjects were being criticized, a variety of individuals and groups (for example, People for Ethical Treatment of Animals) have criticized science and scientists for indifference to the pain and suffering endured by animals used as subjects of research ranging from the imposition of intolerable conditions of crowding on rats and mice to study overcrowding's physiological and behavioral consequences to the use of rabbits, cats, and dogs in testing and evaluating a variety of pharmacological and other products and surgical procedures. Some of the most criticized studies use more highly aware and sentient primates in programs of research on everything from drug addiction to automobile safety, in which they suffer at best from extreme and numbing boredom, and at worst from deliberately imposed physical and psychological trauma. Again, in response to the criticism of many forms of animal experimentation, the issue of animal rights has been established as a significant area of the study of ethics.

An additional ground for developing anti-science attitudes emerges from the apparent necessity of deceiving human subjects in social scientific research. The classic study by Dr. Stanley Milgram of response to authority is a good example. Subjects were told they would be administering painful electric shocks to other subjects in an adjacent room in response to orders given by the experimenter, and that they should pay no attention to responses from the subjects allegedly being shocked. As the apparent subjects cried out in pain with successive increases in voltage, the "confederates" who administered the shocks and who were in reality the subjects of the experiment were observed for the emotional stress induced by being forced to harm fellow humans with increasingly painful shocks. The widespread need to deceive subjects in research of this sort raised serious questions about the ethical and humane standards and moral acceptability of much social scientific research.

THE ENVIRONMENTAL CRITIQUE

Other early sallies in the science wars were fired by participants in the burgeoning environmental movement. Prompted initially by the 1962 publication of Rachel Carson's *The Silent Spring*,[16] environmental advocates began, during the late 1960s, to criticize the apparent indifference of scientists and technologists to the environmental insults of a variety of their activities. Scientists who devised and technologists who manufactured and distributed pesticides and herbicides were the initial targets of these critics, who pointed to the impact of these poisons on wildlife and, through the food chain, on human health. Over time the critique broadened to include problems of storing, using, and disposing of radioactive and other toxic materials. The environmental critique has expanded during the past twenty years to cover recombinant DNA research, which threatened, according to such critics as Jeremy Rifkin, to visit upon us new and potentially uncontrollable organisms.

At the heart of the environmental critique of science lay contrasting visions of the relationship of human beings to the rest of nature. Many environmentalists took a cue from historian Lynn White Jr., who claimed that the Western Judeo-Christian tradition "legitimated the domination of nature by man."[17] By comparison with, for example, the Buddhist tradition that views human beings as integral parts of the entire natural world, the tradition of the West conceived of humans, "created in the image of God," as somehow superior to the rest of nature and free to control and dominate it, violently if necessary. Since humans are given, in the words of the Book of Genesis, "dominion over the fish of the sea, the fowl of the air and over all the earth," the culture of the West felt justified in intruding upon, manipulating, altering, and controlling the flora and fauna of the globe with a species-centric rather than an ecological emphasis. Although environmentalism as a social movement is now eminently respectable and politically correct, the technological and industrial manipulation of the environment and production of invasive products and techniques continues while we debate and worry about such issues as global warming, the hole in the ozone layer, destruction of the tropical rain forest, the despoliation of the ocean and inland waterways with toxic runoff and dumping, and the impact on human health of radioactive products and electromagnetic fields. A perhaps unique aspect of the environmental critique is that many of the critics of the scientific and technological origins of environmental insults are themselves scientists.

THE FEMINIST CRITIQUE

The violence of the human assault on the seas, the air, and the earth and its living products, as pointed out by environmentalists, captured the attention of a particular segment of feminist critics of science, who saw in the depredations on the environment the marks of characteristic male attitudes and behavior. The feminist movement, which until the appearance of eco-feminism had concentrated chiefly on such equity issues as equalizing the opportunities for women to enter the scientific professions and receiving equal pay for equal work and merit, now saw an even more dangerous threat in the dominance in science of such a typically male characteristic as the drive for power and control. As a result, this critique, rather than merely advocating the entry of women into an establishment run by males, began to suggest that the actual doing of science should embrace and reflect such typically feminine attributes as responsiveness, empathy, and gentleness rather than the male ones of forceful domination designed to bend nature to human needs and the human will. This, far more than equity feminism, strikes at the very heart of what science is and how it is done.

THE POLITICAL CRITIQUES

An additional area of criticism of contemporary science emanates from both the left and the right wings of the political spectrum. As long as science was small, relatively powerless politically, and restricted in great part to the ivory towers of the research universities, it was largely unseen and hence inoffensive. But with the growth after the war of Big Science, the name of the game changed. The government created and funded agencies charged with scientific-technological missions, in sharp contrast to the pre-war days when the federal science budget was miniscule and federal policies governing science and technology were, for practical purposes, non-existent. As the recipient of government grants and contracts for the conducting of research, much of it oriented by design to meet policy-determined national needs, the university became an important player in the Big Science game. At the same time, many large corporations, having seen demonstrated during the war the fruitfulness and the profitability of increasing their research budgets, began to engage in both independent corporate research and contracted research designed to make corporate talent available to the government, chiefly in the policy-determined fields of defense, space, and energy.

As kind of mirror images of each other, the political right and left began to see threats in both governmental and corporate scientific activity. Both saw science being captured and co-opted by powerful and fearsome forces. The conservatives perceived the threat of science being used as a weapon by big government to undermine and erode the free marketplace and the rights of individuals and industries. The liberals, on the other hand, feared that the capture of science by the corporate world, both in its own laboratories and in its incursions into the no-longer-so-ivory tower posed comparable threats to the rights and interests of the people. Given these attitudes, it appeared inevitable that the institution of science, as the object of control and manipulation by both government and the corporations, would itself become the subject of political critiques.

As a consequence of the increasingly strident tone of these various criticisms of the changing role of the institution of science and the attitudes, methods, and behavior of scientists, controversies concerning science began to get more exposure in the popular press. As a result, the general public, who had traditionally viewed science as certain, authoritative, benevolent, objective, and universal, began to raise questions about this relatively immaculate image. The press began to document and feature controversies that sometimes pitted scientist against scientist and sometimes scientist against layman. This increased acceptance of the possibility of fallibility and error in science led to openness to alternative views of nature and the physical world and to increased lay acceptance of non-scientific and non-Western ideas and practices, ranging from belief in the reality of extraterrestrials on earth to embracing acupuncture as a universal nostrum. The response of science was, predictably, to warn the public that quacks and charlatans, offering irrational, untested, and unproven ideas and practices, posed both social and medical risks to the public. Scientists pointed to the great public interest and faith in such fraudulent medications as laetrile as evidence that this critique of science could be very costly to the public, both in dollars and in improperly and incompetently treated illness.

Still, society continued to entertain increasing doubts about the infallibility of science and the scientific world view and science's freedom from parochial self-interest. Numerous cases came to light of lay observation of connections between the presence of a variety of toxins in the environment and human health, while scientific spokespersons steadfastly denied the existence of such connections. The growth of this so-called barefoot epidemiology began to cast doubts on the authoritativeness of scientific reassurances and on the neutrality and trustworthiness of scientific experts. Where expertise, as noted by Dixy Lee Ray, had earlier been widely accepted and believed, it now became increasingly suspect, probably because it became ever more difficult to disentangle expertise from vested interest. And a more sophisticated public began to understand that vested interest on the part of experts need not be either hypocritical or venal. Someone trained, for example, as a nuclear engineer has spent years being socialized to and internalizing the conceptual models, attitudes, and dogmas of his or her profession. It is difficult to imagine such a person approaching the question of building more nuclear power plants with Solomon-like neutrality. Once more, the convergence of science and technology, their entanglement with public policy, and the incursions of commerce and industry into the world of scientific research all seem to conspire to undermine the Mertonian norm of disinterestedness.

PEER REVIEW

Given these grounds for increasing public doubt about the authoritativeness of expert opinion, science's traditional and hallowed system of quality control—peer review—came under fire. Chubin and Hackett's 1990 book, *Peerless Science*, highlights some of the criticisms of peer review and considers the questions, raised by some critics, of

> whether "good" and "bad" science can be distinguished, whether science and values can be separated in the course of public decision-making, whether peers can be identified for most scientific work, and whether gatekeepers exercise good faith in their use of peer review. Some critics claim that peer reviewed decisions are based mainly on an ideology which protects the "old boy network" from scrutiny by peers. . . .
>
> Deborah Shapley and Rustum Roy assert that our society's dependence on peer review, which has endured for thirty years, resulted from a combination of arrogance, inertia and fear. A generation of scientists has experienced no other means of obtaining research funding and thus feel their careers at risk whenever questions about peer review are raised.[18]

Chubin and Hackett go on to bemoan the lack of good evidence on the efficacy of peer review as a quality control mechanism and are unimpressed by studies of peer review at the National Institutes of Health and the National Science Foundation that "have generally concluded that peer review operates fairly to identify and support the best science." They go on to cite other studies that "discern in peer review unmistakable bias toward conservatism in the name of quality control." For all these reasons, what had once seemed to be an immaculate and inerrant system of quality control is viewed by Chubin and Hackett, in conformity with the views of other social scientists, as "a social and political process that turns on issues of privacy, efficiency, safety and fairness."

Many of these criticisms of science's institutional modes and practices found warrants in the war in Vietnam in the 1960s and 1970s. Critics of the war made the case that certain segments of the scientific community were in league with a corrupt political-industrial-military establishment in conducting what was increasingly being viewed as a brutal and unjust war of imperialism. The fact that many members of the scientific establishment had gone on record as opposing the war did not appear to diminish the presumed guilt of those scientists and technologists who lent their expertise to the war effort.

THE CREATIONIST CRITIQUE

A final critique of science stems from an area quite distant from those discussed above. This is the critique offered by believers in creationism as the origin of life forms on earth. It was hoped by many, with the 1927 trial of John Scopes in Dayton, Tennessee, that the foundations of anti-evolutionism had been swept away by Clarence Darrow's ridicule, and that public school and college teachers of biology would be free, without pressure from creationists, to teach evolution: the theory of origins universally recognized by the biological community and accepted as the concept that unifies the total spectrum of biological research, from microbiology to ecology. But in 1961 Whitcomb and Morris published *The Genesis Flood*, which relit the flames of controversy and introduced as a more respectable alternative to religion-based creationism what they called scientific creationism.[19] Since the early 1960s the scientific creationist movement appears to have picked up momentum under the leadership of such spokesmen as Duane Gish, author of *Evolution: The Challenge of the Fossil Record*,[20] and Phillip E. Johnson, a professor of law at the University of California, Berkeley, and author of *Darwin on Trial*.[21] Although the social constructivist, radical environmentalist, and eco-feminist groups of critics each have their special and unique critical agendas, it is possible to discern some common threads in their approaches to science. But the scientific creationist critics share little if any of the critical ground of these other groups, and their appearance during the time when other criticisms of science were surfacing appears to be little more than happenstance.

Nevertheless, despite the lack of commonality between the creationist critique and those reflecting post-modern thought, either in fundamental assumptions or in the populations espousing these views, the sense that criticisms of science's epistemology, methods, and orientation were arising on all sides prompted some members of the scientific establishment to rise up against their critics during the 1990s. For the three decades since the early 1960s, apart from an occasional response from leaders or spokespersons of the scientific community in such journals as *Science*, scientists tended to ignore what most of them perceived as ignorant, ill-founded, and unwarranted attacks on them and their professional activities. Indeed, there appeared to be little need to defend a profession that had contributed so obviously and so richly to the quality of life, intellectual as well as material, in the post–World War II era, especially in the West, where most of the criticisms originated. And as long as the criticisms tended to appear in specialized literary, philosophical, or social scientific journals with little popular readership there seemed to be little reason for scientists to use their valuable time to defend their raison d'etre. But as the popular press began to pay more attention to the critics of science, it became evident to some scientists that their profession might be beginning to lose some of the high credibility it had enjoyed for many decades. And with this loss of credibility came the potential for reduction of public funding, which had to be provided by a Congress sensitive to changes in the currents of popular opinion. How great an erosion of credibility had science suffered as a result of the doubts and questions raised by its critics? No one really knew, but by the early 1990s it became apparent that some scientists felt sufficiently threatened that they were impelled to go public with a defense of the rationality and the benevolence of science and an attack on what they viewed as uninformed, biased, and unwarranted criticism.

THE SCIENCE WARS

The issue was really joined in 1994 with the publication of *Higher Superstition: The Academic Left and its Quarrels with Science*, by Paul Gross, a biologist at the University of Virginia, and Norman Levitt, a mathematician at Rutgers University.[22] This volume, while concentrating on refuting the epistemological analyses of what the authors call "the academic left," undertakes to show the flaws in the broad critiques of science offered by eco-feminists and radical environmentalists, as well as demonstrating the fallacies of the positions of radical AIDS activists, Afrocentric "science," and radical animal rights activists, while touching only lightly on the creationist critique originating in the Institute for Creation Research and on what its authors would characterize as other assorted silliness, such as astrology.

Writing in a slashing critical style, Gross and Levitt castigate the critics and opponents of science chiefly for their ignorance of the very subject of their criticism: science. As its subtitle suggests, the villains, in the view of Gross and Levitt, are members of the academic left: the deconstructionist, social constructivist, anti-rational, and post-modern literary and cultural critics. Even given the sweeping and often eloquent analyses of Gross and Levitt, the issue of science and anti-science didn't really hit the streets until the May 1996 publication of a hoax article, "Transgressing the Boundaries: The Transformative Hermeneutics of Quantum Gravity," in the leftist cultural studies journal *Social Text*.[23] The author of this article, New York University physics professor Alan Sokal, used the language and style of social constructivism and cultural studies to write a parodic article of the purest and most inspired nonsense. The issue of *Social Text* in which the Sokal article appeared was a special one, devoted to analysis of the science wars and intended, in the words of Gross and Levitt, "to vindicate assorted post-structuralist, multicultural and feminist critiques of science and to denounce their critics, most notably the depraved Gross and Levitt."

Within days of the publication of the Sokal article, the journal *Lingua Franca* published Sokal's revelation of the hoax he had perpetrated.[24] For perhaps the first time, the issue of the science wars, formerly joined largely in the rarefied precincts of the ivory tower, became the subject of wide coverage in the popular press. In the meantime, along with such scientific, historical, and philosophical eminences as Loren Fishman, Susan Haack, Gerald Holton, and Martin Lewis, Gross and Levitt became part of a committee that organized a 1996 conference called "The Flight from Science and Reason," under the auspices of the New York Academy of Sciences. During the course of this conference some forth-five scientists, philosophers, historians, and social scientists undertook to refute a wide range of cultural criticisms of science. Henry Greenberg, of the New York Academy, suggested in the introductory remarks to the proceedings of the conference that it arose "out of the primary concerns of the hard physical and biological sciences," and concentrated on "the threats to these disciplines." The chief issues under discussion, again in Greenberg's words, "relate to scientific reasoning, logical deduction and professional expertise."[25]

The participants in this conference took aim at a wide assortment of irrational and un- or anti-scientific attitudes and behaviors. Among them are feminist epistemology, creationism, radical environmentalism, African history and pseudo-science, the alternative medicine movement, "voodoo" sociology of science, and a full range of other movements they viewed as intellectual charlatanage. The papers ranged from muted and quietly reasoned arguments to polemical diatribes, for instance the essay by Mario Bunge called "Charlatanism in Academia," in which he asserts that

> the academic charlatans have not earned the academic freedom they enjoy nowadays. They have not earned it because they produce or circulate cultural garbage, which is not just a nonacademic activity but an antiacademic one. Let them do that anywhere else they please, but not in schools; for these are supposed to be places of learning. We should expel the charlatans from the university before they deform it out of recognition and crowd out the serious searchers for truth. They should be criticized, nay denounced, with the same rigor and vigor that Julien Benda attacked the intellectual mercenaries of his time in his memorable *La trahison des clercs*—which, incidentally, earned him the hatred of the so-called organic intellectuals of all political hues. Spare the rod and spoil the charlatan. Spoil the charlatan and put modern culture at risk. Jeopardize modern culture and undermine modern civilization. Debilitate modern civilization and prepare for a new Dark Age.[26]

Strong words!

In a defensive move against these recently aroused and activated scientists and supporters of science, Andrew Ross, editor of *Social Text*, edited and published in 1996 an expanded version of the papers that were published in the special edition of *Social Text* in which the Sokal hoax had appeared. The book, called *Science Wars*, omits the Sokal piece. In his introduction, Ross decries the "climate of caricature" established by the Gross and Levitt book and maintains, in most reasonable terms, that the cultural critics and social constructivists have no wish to destroy or undermine science, but wish merely to demystify and demythologize the conduct of science. He characterizes four possible political aims of critiquing groups:

> a) some simply want to provide an accurate, scientific description of empirical scientific practice; b) others want, more ambitiously, to see science redeem its tarnished ideals from internal abuse and external impurities; c) others, more normative, would persuade scientists to be more self-critical about the political nature and social origins of their research and to engage in advocacy science to combat the risks and injustices that are side-effects of technoscientific development; d) still others want, more radically, to create new scientific methods that are rooted in the social needs of communities and accountable to social interests other than those of managerial elites in business, government and the military. The last aim is driven by the principle that people whose lives are greatly affected by the effects of scientific superindustrialism ought to have a role in the decision making that determines research. But it also involves taking seriously the proposition that Western technoscience is a highly local form of knowledge and is therefore unlikely to have a world monopoly on good scientific ideas.[27]

Thus, the most verbal adversaries in the science wars have taken their positions and, in the words of Langdon Winner, now "the gloves come off." The intransigence of the positions taken by the antagonists and the vehemence with which their views are expressed would lead an observer to conclude that much of Western culture is at stake and that, therefore, the arguments must be reverberating throughout the scientific and lay communities.

And yet we have been surprised, in the course of many conversations with many colleagues, friends, and acquaintances both within and outside of academia, by the lack of interest in and information about what appears to be a titanic intellectual struggle. Not only did we sense that the science wars are not a burning issue; we also observed that many thoughtful and generally well-informed people are almost totally unaware of them. If this is indeed the case, the dismal predictions of the Grosses, Levitts, and Bunges would appear to be quite incommensurate with the problem. On the other hand, our impressions were simply that: casual and informal observations that could be skewed and misleading. Despite our impressions to the contrary, it is possible that our technoscientific culture, to which we owe so much in terms of intellectual and physical well-being, is being systematically subverted by a latter-day irrational barbarism. We decided, therefore, in a modest way, to try to assess the extent of the "attack" on science and reason and to estimate the damage being done to our society by the science wars.

PLAN OF RESEARCH

If the "golden age" image of science in 1960 has indeed been transformed into an image of "science under siege," as a result of the criticism of various feminist, environmentalist, social constructivist, creationist, and politically liberal and conservative groups, what can we discover about the extent, the intensity, and the social implications of these attacks? Since our knowledge of these criticisms is drawn largely from the writings of a small number of highly visible and public spokespersons, we know very little about whether or not these views are shared by other, more local and grassroots members of the critical groups. In other words, are the so-called science wars contained within the select and vocal circles of particular circles of academe or are they also evident in the population at large? And do members of groups known for their anti-science sentiments cut a wide swath of criticism across the discipline or are their complaints limited to issues that pertain specifically to their special interests?

Therefore, in this exploratory research, we attempt to move beyond simply identifying the science critics and their arguments to provide a theoretically informed account of what may be involved in the science wars. It is our contention that there are at least two possible basic explanations for the apparent recent increase in criticism of science. The first is a societal-level explanation that focuses on the erosion of confidence in and support for a wide array of social institutions, including science. The second is an organizational-political-level explanation that focuses on the growth and activities of interest groups with specific policy agendas that may touch upon science, or with specific critiques of corporate or governmental power that have co-opted science as a servant of these powers. Let us discuss each of these explanations in turn.

GENERAL CYNICISM

In 1966 the Lou Harris poll asked a national sample of Americans how they felt about a number of major social institutions such as the Congress, the presidency, labor unions, the medical profession, major corporations, and eight others. At the extremes, about 72 percent of the respondents had "a great deal of confidence" in the medical profession while only 22 percent felt the same way about labor unions. Overall, however, the proportion of Americans expressing a great deal of confidence across all thirteen social institutions was about 50 percent. When that poll was repeated in 1984, the proportion expressing a like level of confidence across all the institutions dropped to 31 percent. And when the same poll was conducted in 1988 in a small Indiana town with relatively high unemployment, the percentage saying they had "a great deal of confidence" dropped to 17 percent.[28]

Although respondents were not asked specifically about science as a social institution in the original poll or either of its two iterations, it is certainly possible that there would have been a decline in confidence in this area as well as the thirteen others. Science, like all other institutions, has had its share of public scandals that have eroded public trust. Just as Watergate and other political scandals have tarnished the image of political institutions, the ethical shortcomings of scientists, exposed in events involving plagiarism, fabrication of results, and putting subjects at severe risk in medical experiments, may have put science's good name at risk. In short, has science been perceived as being in step with other corrupted social institutions, resulting in the expression of decreasing confidence in them by a growing proportion of Americans? If this is true, we may conclude that we have gone from a situation of largely trusting our institutions and leaders in the early 1960s to one of believing cynically that social institutions are all about self-interest, with "every devil for himself."

If this explanation is accurate and there is, in fact, a general trend of increased cynicism and mistrust of institutions among the American public, we must conclude that science is not being singled out for special criticism, but simply is being painted with the same broad brush of cynicism that is being directed at a variety of other institutions. Thus, the alleged critics of science among feminists or environmentalists would be seen not as expressing narrow, parochial views, but rather as giving voice to criticisms of science as one of many increasingly mistrusted social institutions.

INTEREST GROUP ACTIVISM

But there is an alternative explanation for science's fallen stock. In recent decades there has been a shift from people's involvement in mass organizations like labor unions or other class-based interest groups to greater participation in single-issue activist organizations or groups where membership is based on fixed status characteristics. This shift is reflected in the move from class politics to identity politics. The identity may be based on gender, race, ethnicity, sexual orientation, physical condition, or single-minded commitment to specific social goals. The combination of identity politics and single-issue interest groups has produced a proliferation of national interest groups seeking to shape the economic, political, and social agendas of the nation.

The goals, interests, and ideologies of interest groups focusing on women's issues, the environment, and religion are often directly affected by the activities of science. Women's groups are concerned about the receptiveness of the profession to female practitioners and how medical science deals with specific gender-related health issues such as breast cancer. Environmental activists are concerned about the effects of scientific research and science-based technology on global warming and the ozone layer or about the environmental effects of deforestation. Religious fundamentalists are concerned about the work of evolutionary biologists that challenges the biblical account of creation. Each of the groups sees and evaluates the work of scientists through the lens of its own interests and ideologies. Each interest group may attack science for its actions (or non-actions) that affect their group, without necessarily developing a wide-ranging critique of science. Thus, an interest group perspective would lead one to expect that each interest group will be critical of science on matters that most directly affect its agenda, but will be less critical—or not critical at all—of science at it affects the agendas of other interest groups.

If the General Cynicism hypothesis were confirmed by the research, our basic question about the origins and the grounds for the growing anti-science sentiment would be answered. All social institutions would be seen as equally under attack because of the widespread reporting of incompetence, dishonesty, or malfeasance of their members. If, however, this hypothesis were not confirmed and the research suggested that the interest group activism hypothesis offered a better explanation of the more evident recent critiques of science, a second question would present itself: How widely within various interest groups are anti-science sentiments distributed? Do these criticisms represent the views of large numbers of rank-and-file members of the feminist, environmentalist, and other groups, or are they merely the opinions of a relatively small number of nationally or internationally visible and self-appointed leaders and spokespersons?

ASSESSING THE ALTERNATIVE THEORETICAL VIEWS

In order to assess the relative validity of the General Cynicism and Interest Group Activism hypotheses, we sampled sixty people, ten from each of five groups alleged to be critical of science and ten from a group assumed to be unaffected by the actions of science. The people selected for interviews were as follows:

1. Feminists—Ten female Ph.D. holders (one was a Ph.D. candidate) with appointments or affiliations with a women's studies program or a women's caucus at a major university.
2. Environmentalists—Ten persons who have leadership positions or who play active roles in local chapters of national environmental organizations (e.g., the Audubon Society, the Sierra Club), or in local/regional environmental action groups. Many of those selected have advanced degrees in science-related fields.
3. Religious fundamentalists (creationists)—Ten pastors of fundamentalist churches, identified and selected by a scholar of denominational differences in belief and commitment, from a list of all local religious organizations.
4. Political left—Ten leaders or very active members of national political organizations guided by socialist principles on matters of production and distribution of goods and services, and by "progressive" principles on a variety of social issues.
5. Political right—Ten leaders or very active members of local conservative groups. Most are frequent authors of very conservative columns or letters to the editor in the local press.
6. General sample—In order to have a "control group," we selected ten persons holding leadership positions in local organizations that appear to be relatively unaffected by the work of science, chiefly organizations devoted to the arts and related cultural activities. The members of this group are as prominent and as well-educated as persons from the other five groups, but their organizations have goals and interests that fall outside the direct influence of scientific knowledge and practice.

These sixty persons were contacted for interviews, and fifty-eight interviews actually took place. The interviews lasted for between one and two hours and were recorded. Topics covered included: (a) background in and experiences with various areas of science; (b) general views of the contributions of science; (c) the role of women in science; (d) how science and science-based technology have affected the environment; (e) the historical and evolving relation of science to government and private corporations; and (f) science and religion, with special attention to creation science. The interviews were semi-structured, permitting interviewers to probe answers with follow-up questions. After the interviews, all respondents were asked to complete a questionnaire with pre-coded attitude items. These items are related to the topics covered in the interviews and allow for comparison across the six groups on more standardized questions.

It should be clear that our sample was selected purposively and is not representative of a specified larger population. The feminists, fundamentalists, and so on were selected because of their level of activism in local interest groups, and not on the basis of random selection. However, in selecting our sample, our goal was to obtain coverage of a range of organizations that, on a national level, have been involved in disputes with science.

We analyzed the interview and questionnaire data obtained from these six groups in order to assess the relative validity of our two theoretical alternatives. There is, of course, a third possibility: that the respondents of the six groups are neither very critical of or cynical about science in general, nor of science as it relates to the specific goals and ideologies of their interest groups. Thus, neither of our alternative explanations of the science wars would be supported, and our findings would suggest that different views of science are held by a small number of nationally visible spokespersons for these groups and by the rank-and-file members of the groups who are active at the local level. If this were the case, the so-called science wars could be viewed as mostly media-driven, expressing the views of a small national elite group and with little foundation in the experiences of the local level activists. This finding would lead to the conclusion that neither of our explanations is valid, and that the science wars are no more than the rarefied opinions of small and relatively uninfluential minorities.

On the one hand, the General Cynicism hypothesis would receive support if there is a high degree of similarity in the criticisms of science that are expressed across the six groups of respondents, criticisms that reflect low popular confidence in most social institutions. This would indicate that there may be widespread suspicion of science across many different organized segments of opinion leaders. Such a situation would reflect an important shift in support for science and might signal growing dissatisfaction with science as one of many social institutions about which large segments of the public are cynical.

On the other hand, if the Interest Group Activism perspective has validity, we would expect the respondents from each group to criticize science mainly in the areas of concern to their groups. Thus, we would expect feminists to be concerned mainly with matters related to how science affects women, and to be less interested in and even supportive of science on matters related to the environment, religion, or politics. Similarly, we would expect religious fundamentalists to be critical of science on matters related to creationism versus evolution, but neutral toward or even supportive of science in discussing matters such as the environment or women in science. Because of the breadth and comprehensiveness of their critiques, the views of the extreme left and the extreme right might be expected to be most critical of science in general, but even they should emphasize those aspects of science most inimical to their particular interests and views.

Reflections of a Feminist

"When I came of age in the 1970s in San Francisco, I didn't even know anyone who wasn't a feminist. It was kind of in the air that you breathe."

My natal family is really conservative. My mother was a stay-at-home housewife her whole life and she had accepted the kinds of choices I made in fairly good grace, but she certainly wasn't supportive.

By the time I entered graduate school in the mid-1970s people were reading feminist books and talking about feminist ideas. But more to the point, they were structuring relationships, careers, and families in very feminist ways. It was not something that required soul-searching because there was a lot of support for people who were saying, "If you're going to live with someone he sure as hell better do his share of the dishes." And once you started to contemplate having kids, obviously you wouldn't want to do that unless the person you were going to do it with was actively engaged as a co-parent.

Although my background was conservative, there was no culture shock when I encountered feminism because the whole process was fairly gradual. By the time you were really ready to talk about the heavy issues like, "I wonder if I'll ever have kids," you have been dealing with little issues for a long time.

I think that there are certain bonds between feminism and environmentalism. For me, it was part of the lefty lifestyle that had a sort of organic connection between the anti-war movement and the beginnings of the feminist movement. I certainly know feminists today who are environmentalists, but I also know people who get into their gas-guzzling SUVs and off they go without thinking twice about it. There is a movement on campus now to get people to boycott gas in order to get big oil to bring down the price. They want lower gas prices, which is really about let's consume, consume, consume. The people circulating the boycott idea don't get it at all! And I'm sure some of them are feminists. So maybe in the 1970s there was an organic or inevitable connection between feminism and environmentalism, but I don't see feminists today being environmentalists or vice versa.

One thing that may link feminists and environmentalists is a concern about issues of control and power. There is a challenge to patriarchal power and wanting women to have more control over their lives and more voice in public decision making. And there is a certain kind of feminism, maybe feminism at its best, that is asking whether we want to think about any relationships in terms of dominion at all, whether over people or the environment. And there is a kind of environmentalism that is concerned with the tendency to see Man, with a capital *M*, as the center of the universe, shaping everything to our needs.

Generally speaking, I would like the society we live in to be more just in terms of income distribution and social relations. I think we should be going in the direction of Brazilian society, where people have interesting physical features without being clearly European or clearly Asian, or African, but a kind of interesting combination. My ideal for society and the kinds of things that I work for have a lot to do with making the division of labor more fluid—the division between working outside the home or inside the home, caring for children versus caring for income. I think that generally people ought to be responsible for both needs, because that is what a really satisfying life should be. The majority of families have partners that work outside the home, but in the majority of families the men don't do very much of the work of reproducing life. I don't know if my vision is for a more androgynous approach to how we deal with families and home, or just to be more flexible, which is what my students always say. A woman who is ambitious and wants to go out to work should do that. The ones into nurturing and caring, a great cook and good with the details, should stay home and take care of the house. I think its has to be more than that. Flexibility of choice still leaves us with intact gender signals about what we ought to be doing. I'm interested in ways to encourage nurturing fathers.

I think that science can make a contribution to building a better society, and I know that scholarly research can have a terrific impact. I see it as one way of being a kind of activist. But science and technology means more than just crunching and computers, and B. F. Skinner and those conditioning experiments, it also includes things like qualitative social-science research. Carefully done research that requires us to think critically about our social conditions can be very helpful. I'm thinking about Carol Gilligan's work when she was challenging Lawrence Kohlberg's stuff on child development and moral sensibilities. She decided that she would look at the development of moral voices in young women students as opposed to young men students. I think that has been very significant research that has changed the way that we think about human moral development.

I know that some areas of research have become controversial, like DNA research and testing on fetal tissue. The fetal tissue stuff doesn't bother me. Some of the recombinant DNA research does trouble me, such as the human genome project and its potential to satisfy the desires of some people for designer babies. You produce a child with the sex you want, the IQ you want, perfect features, no defects or whatever you would define as a defect. I don't think that is a good idea—engineering diversity away, anything that is less than ideal. I just don't think that sounds like a smart idea. I think there are reasons that genetic selection has occurred the way it has, and human intervention can sort of screw things up, so that the right features are not resistant to diseases.

Religion is one of those things I feel deeply ambivalent about. Religious traditions have bolstered my life, my deeply felt feelings, the notion of conscience and what a person should do with their life, and notions of social justice. I have found religion to be supportive and important in my life. It's like a support—the 1960s, '70s thing. Religious folk and religious institutions helped bolster fights against homophobia and for more economic justice. On the other hand, I'm not deeply oriented toward religion. I go to church, I sing in the church choir, my children go to church. There is a community of people that matters to me, people who put together community aid marches, who organize against the KKK. But in this community I am aware that religion comes in many shapes and sizes. There are some religious folks who are bigots and they have nothing to do with me. There are other religious folks who see themselves as driven by religious motivations, who are really struggling with a kind of narrow traditionalism found in conservative evangelical Christian churches. So religion can be a positive force, and I guess I want my kids exposed to it. I want them to have something they can rebel against if they want to. If I'm really honest about it, a whole lot of the dogma stuff is silly, and it's probably more social than it is religion. I don't think of God as creator, our father. I think of God as this image we have made for ourselves. I know that's an odd way of looking at it, but it's what makes sense to me.

The last twenty years have seen increasing skepticism and nervousness about science, but it seems to me that the public still views science as basically helpful. The skepticism comes from stories about the Y2K bug, counting keystrokes in the workplace, or invading people's privacy. But people are not being very critical, because science is always beneficial and scientists always know what they are doing. A lot of criticism is generated among people who are knowledgeable about what goes on in research on fetal tissue, the human genome. But my general sense is that most Americans still think of science as capital *GT*—good thing.

I don't include myself in this positive view of science, because there are too many things that we do in a half-assed way in this country. We don't have decent mass transit. What we have are people who think of their automobiles as an extension of themselves. We don't have bike lanes or decent little paths along the river that are available for twenty-mile rides or runs. No, we have made some really disastrous and stupid decisions about technology in this country, particularly because we have accepted the individual's right to get around with the internal combustion engine, which is stupid. Sure, it's a big country, but we can have decent transportation in town for students who think it is their God-given right to park on campus. I could get going on this, but my skepticism goes to the kind of thing we do at the daily level, the policies and decisions made in this country that keep gas cheap and encourage people to rely on cars wherever they go. In Japan, no one would think of climbing in a car to drive from Tokyo to Kyoto. It's nuts, but it is really more policy and political than science and technology.

I think that it's important to bring an informed skepticism to the work of science. There aren't any clear and compelling answers about a lot of things. I don't think that science's way of knowing is unique, because observation and experimentation are part of learning in every field. Scientific knowledge may be more reliable because well-done, careful experimentation leads to more reliable results than haphazard, careless, poorly designed experimentation. But it wouldn't guarantee that you're getting reliable knowledge.

I don't know whether scientific knowledge should be more privileged than knowledge gained by other means. If I were designing a raft to get me across a body of water and I had some blueprints on how to put a raft together, and then someone who has done a lot of work on rafts told me how to put the pieces together, I think I would rely on that person more heavily than someone who said he would think about how to build a raft. But just because scientists figure out the nuts and bolts of how to do something, I don't think their knowledge should serve as the guide to whether we should use it. So maybe in some certain limited context, scientific knowledge should be more privileged, but we should be very clear about the context.

Chapter 2

The Feminist Voice

Problems of a Male-Dominated Science

A number of analysts expressing concern about the widespread "attacks" on science in contemporary literature have pointed to feminist scholars and writers as a source of the sharpest criticism of science today. They are even characterized by some as anti-science, in that they reject science as a way of knowing and actively call for something different.

Our feminist respondents do not appear to warrant the anti-science label, in the sense that they either fail to recognize the contributions and potential benefits of science or call for the displacement of science from its place in academe or other institutional centers of influence. We would expect the feminists to be amused by, but not endorse, the following satiric statement by the novelist Kurt Vonnegut speaking to the graduating class of 1970 at Bennington College.

We would be a lot safer if the government would take its money out of science and put it into astrology and the reading of palms. I used to think that science would save us, and science certainly tried. But we can't stand any more tremendous explosions, either for or against democracy. Only in superstition is there hope. If you want to become a friend of civilization, then become an enemy of truth, and a fanatic for harmless balderdash. . . . I beg you to believe in the most ridiculous superstition of them all: that humanity is at the center of the universe, the fulfiller and the frustrator of the grandest dreams of god Almighty.

About astrology and palmistry: they are good because they make people feel vivid and full of possibilities. They are communism at its best. Everybody has a birthday and almost everybody has a palm. Take a seemingly drab person born on August 3rd, for instance. He is a Leo. He is proud, generous, trusting, energetic, domineering, and authoritative! All Leos are! He is ruled by the Sun! His genes are the ruby and diamond! His color is orange! His metal is gold! This is a *nobody?* . . . Ask him to show you his amazing palms. What a fantastic heart line he has! Be on your guard, girls. Have you ever seen a Hill of the Moon like this? Wow! This is some human being![1]

37

Rather than being rejectionists, feminists reveal a kind of "healthy skepticism" that some analysts of science view as central to the value system of science. That said, however, it must be noted that the feminist commentary on science is wide-ranging, revealing concerns and questions about science that might be taken as a "slashing critique" by the average biologist, physicist, or medical researcher.

When discussing whether science has made life better or worse in their lifetime, most of the women are unequivocal about their belief that life is better: advances in medical science, increased life expectancy, material goods, computers, space travel. However, four of the respondents acknowledge contributions while they provided extensive comment on science's potential for damaging the environment and on undesirable consequences for quality of life, while recognizing that these effects may not be science per se, but its technological applications.

Just as the results of science are seen as neither all good nor all bad, our respondents have a matter-of-fact reaction to the tendency of scientists to publicly disagree on a broad range of topics such as global warming or nutrition. Such disagreements in scientific analysis or reversals in scientific findings (e.g., first butter is harmful to health and then it's not) do not lead feminists to be turned off from paying attention to what scientists report in the media. Quite the opposite!

- "I take an intellectual interest in their disagreements. . . . I'm not troubled by it."
- "My first reaction is, I'm glad to hear disagreements because I know that people are truly searching for answers. The questions are complex and our perception of things changes over the years. I think it's a healthy problem."
- "When it comes to global warming or holes in the ozone layer, I have kind of Sierra Club reaction—caution. Maybe scientists aren't correct, but the dangers are so serious and irreversible that we better pay attention."
- "I take a wait-and-see attitude and watch for more information on the subject."

For some, disagreements among scientists tend to reinforce aspects of their critical views of science. Feminists inclined to a post-modern view of knowledge applaud disagreements as support for arguments opposed to the search for definitive knowledge, or truth with a capital *T*.

- "It [disagreements among scientists] confirms my belief that many scientific findings are subject to different interpretations."

- "As long as someone is trying to stake out a position of the truth—thank God someone disagrees."

For others, disagreements are linked to the politics of knowledge in terms of who funds research and how it is conducted. This view of how knowledge is produced in science is a clear challenge to those who believe in the objectivity of science and its methods.

- "When I read about disagreements among scientists, I want to know who funds them, endorses them, and how their research was done."
- "Depends on which scientists. Science is not a uniform field. There are a lot of very corrupted, self-interested scientists and a lot of dedicated, honest scientists. I don't have overall confidence that they are either truthful or disinterested or committed to bettering human life. On a blanket basis they are pretty patriarchal about who does it and how it is done, and they don't understand the ways in which their scientific work is biased. . . . That's fairly general across the field, regardless of whether they are honest, dedicated, or not."

All of the feminist respondents are connected with a university, six as faculty, two as administrators, and one as a graduate student. They have direct experience with the publish-or-perish culture that exists at research universities and with the continuing pressure on faculty to seek funding from federal agencies and private foundations for their research and scholarly activities. This common experience appears to shape their reactions to reports of misconduct by scientists in their work-related activities. Feminists discuss their awareness of a variety of publicly reported cases of falsifying data, misleading subjects, or conducting harmful experiments, but their remarks do not reflect intense anger or shock.

- "Misconduct occurs because of competition for personal gain and a system of intense competitive pressure that makes money, power, and prestige the pre-eminent goals in the lives of scientists."
- "Sometimes it's honest mistakes, but mostly it's driven by competition with other scientists."
- "It is both an individual thing—a highly egocentric personality—and part of a system of publish or perish."
- "It's all about publishing, about getting your name out there."

Given the awareness of scientists' misconduct, what is the role of professional ethics in serving to inhibit such behavior? Are scientists sensitive to the ethical implications of their work? "I don't think they all are. They are not well trained to think about ethical dimensions of their work," said one respondent, and several others also noted that their education does not focus on such matters. Several other respondents stressed that the way in which scientists carry out their work precludes ethical considerations. One stated, "I think that their approach to their inquiry is motivated by concerns that have little to do with ethics." Another said, "They are aware of ethical issues, but when they have strong self-interest in their line of work they will develop rationalizations to deal with ethical issues. They will pose issues as being of competing values: Do you want to use pesticides to produce more food, or let people go hungry?" Finally, a third noted a broader societal responsibility for the way science has been allowed to develop: "No, they are not sensitive to ethical issues, not because they are unethical, but because of the way we treat science—as detached from the social context of their work."

This discussion of scientists' "trained indifference" to ethical issues appears to be similar to how other professionals develop an "incapacity" for considering matters that would distract them from their central purpose. Writer Lillian Ross recently published her memoirs that recounted her forty years as the other "wife" of the longtime editor of *The New Yorker*. The memoir recounts details of two households and the time divided between them, carried out as conventional domestic routines with the full knowledge of all participants. When Ross was asked by an interviewer about whether she had thought about the book's impact on the surviving wife, now in her nineties, she replied, "That isn't the way one thinks when one is a writer. You don't think about what the impact is going to be on other people. You think about what you're writing."[2]

Let us now turn to consider how feminists view science in relation to specific topics such as the environment, women, politics, and religion.

NATURE, SCIENCE, AND CITIZENS: WHAT IS THE BALANCE?

All respondents were asked a series of questions concerning threats to the environment and the role of scientists and citizens in responding to those threats. We expected that answers to these questions would permit us to identify respondents who see the environment as under attack from a prevailing ideology justifying the control or domination of nature for human purposes. This ideology is often viewed as stemming from the scientific attitude toward nature—to learn of its mysteries in order to produce new medicines, new products, or new advances in the way people live. Respondents were also given the opportunity to choose radical or gradual changes as the solution to environmental problems, and to choose to place their trust in the hands of scientists or concerned citizens when dealing with the environment. Thus, we expected to see if any of our respondents exhibited qualities of the "radical environmentalist" discussed by Levitt and Gross—those who seek a harmony with nature, see radical change as essential to save the ecosystem, and point the finger at the unrestrained appetite for scientific research as the source of the problem.

All of the feminist respondents are aware of the dilemma posed by trying to choose between a "passive" science that stresses knowledge about the natural world and an "active" science that pursues application. They are evenly divided in the ways they choose to express their views about the dilemma. One cluster of respondents seems to accept the need for a balance between an active and passive science.

- "It has to be somewhere in the middle. There is emphasis on preserving the natural world, the environment. However, we have to be honest and recognize how we have benefited from the work of science. It has added to our comfort, our standard of living. I think it is the responsibility of scientists, that for any invention they come up with for people's comfort, that it doesn't obviously hurt the environment."
- "The purpose of science is to discover new knowledge, and if there are applications that's okay."
- "Neither the [passive nor active science] would be my answer. The first is a desirable goal, but it's not enough just to sit in the laboratory. To say we should modify nature says that we have a right to manipulate everything else."

Another cluster of respondents chooses not to accept a balance between theory and application, and instead stresses the need for science to accommodate to nature.

- "Science needs to be in balance with nature, so that we don't run out of resources."
- "The objective of science is to learn about nature, and not to control it. In the long run, learning about nature will lead to better balance rather than trying to dominate."
- "The desire to control nature is dangerous. The Eastern way is to be at one with nature, but the Western way is control. Sometimes I wish we would back up a little to the Eastern."

Despite this division among feminist respondents regarding an active or passive role for science, they are almost unanimous in endorsing a combination of radical and gradual approaches to dealing with environmental problems and in calling for scientists and citizens to "work together" toward solving problems. Although attracted to some radical solutions for reducing energy consumption, they shy away from strong recommendations for these uses because "they are not realistic" or a gradual approach is "more feasible," or "it would be wrong to force changes without reconceptualizing how we have organized society" (i.e., you can't limit auto use without rethinking the design of cities, suburbs, and work locations). It is significant to note that although feminists are critical of science's role in creating environmental problems, they do not wish to exclude science from the search for solutions. Scientists and concerned citizens have to be involved in a "partnership," in a "dialogue that brings interaction between them."

Thus, although science and scientists are viewed as implicated in a variety of actions that produce damage to the environment, feminist respondents are not prepared to "throw out the baby with the bathwater." Perhaps because everyone will ultimately lose if there is substantial damage to the ecosystem, there was less finger pointing and more calls for inclusiveness and joint responsibility for environmental problems. It may be that this issue has less salience for feminists, as was suggested in chapter 1 when we discussed the Interest Group Activism hypothesis of reactions to science.

WOMEN AND SCIENCE: PAST, PRESENT, AND FUTURE

All of the feminist respondents are involved in organizations that seek to advance the interests of women within the university and in the larger society. Almost all of them are directly involved in teaching and research concerning women's issues. They were asked three questions about women and science: What have been the implications of a male-dominated science? What can we expect to occur with the recent greater participation of women in science? Will women scientists differ from their male colleagues? Lurking behind these questions is (1) the attempt to uncover the nature of women's grievances against science that are linked to how women have been treated by science, and (2) the attempt to see if feminists expect women scientists to be different simply because they are women (sometimes referred to as an essentialist view of women).

All of our respondents seem to think the implications of a male-dominated science should be obvious, but when asked to be specific they invariably focused on medical research and the selection of subjects and topics for research.

- "Subjects of research were always male, and they tried to adapt the findings to women—and they weren't always valid."
- "Emphasis has been on health issues of more interest to men."
- "Why wasn't breast cancer taken seriously? Why isn't there a male birth control pill?"

- "Medical research has been an area where there have been male blinders."

In addition to the alleged biases in medical research topics, there was mention of the "overwhelmingly greater emphasis on industrial technology and agribusiness technology" and the tendency to follow a "masculine approach to what the world is about," evidenced by the attention to space travel and weapons development.

Feminist respondents are somewhat optimistic about what to expect from the recent increase in the number of women entering scientific fields. There is the obvious hope that women scientists will address some of the neglected topics noted above, and that women will raise the public's consciousness of important health issues. In addition to new topics, there is an inadequately articulated belief that women will make an important difference in the way science is conducted.

- "I think the way scientists validate their topics will change."
- "Women will emphasize the quality of experience. Methodologically, there are subtle differences, reflected in qualitative versus statistical approaches. The feminist perspective is also to work with subjects cooperatively, rather than controlling them."

Several respondents presented a broader, and perhaps more sophisticated, analysis of what might follow from an increase in the number of women scientists. The comments examine the relationship between increasing participation of women in science and the institutional setting in which the work of scientists is conducted.

- "It will be a very long time before an increase in women scientists has much impact. Numbers are not sufficient to have impact in the short term. For example, the former Soviet Union had large numbers of doctors, scientists, and engineers. This had some effect, especially in medicine, but they still developed nuclear weapons. The point is that the professions themselves are so structured patriarchally in their professional values and ideas, even a large number of women will not change this. Because women are not in the most prestigious, most highly rewarded ranks of the professions, it doesn't matter if you have a large number or increasing numbers of women. There needs to be more fundamental changes."
- "Potentially, increased numbers would have no effect. Just because someone is a woman doesn't mean that she will see the world any differently than the dominant society, which is based on a male perspec-

tive. She has to learn to see the world as a male in order to become a scientist."

The apparent lack of strong optimism associated with the growing number of women in science seems to carry over to ambivalent responses to the question of whether women scientists will do science differently than their male colleagues. Our respondents' answers to this question cannot avoid the long-standing controversy in the literature on gender regarding whether and how women differ from men. Half of the respondents make the point that the question, as posed, can draw them into the "essentialist" trap. By and large, they do not believe that women scientists qua women will do different science, but they appear to embrace a view linking women's socialization to doing science differently.

- "Yes, women scientists will be different. Males want control and objectivity, but they are so objective that we remove parts of ourselves that influence the data. Differences are probably due to socialization."
- "I'm not an essentialist, but because of socialization they may choose different topics. The experience of inhabiting their own bodies will encourage women to ask different questions than male scientists."
- "I can envision different projects, not the individualistic, competitive pattern that often takes place."
- "Yes, women will sometimes be different, but not all the time. Women who have a conscious feminist view clearly are doing something different. [Evelyn Fox] Keller's work on [Barbara] McClintock says that she approached biology in a way that men do not."
- "Do I believe the presence of testes or ovaries leads to a different way of doing science? No, I do not. But that doesn't mean I think gender is not important. Gender is very important, but I don't think it is an essential characteristic of science or scientific endeavor."
- "This is a disputed area for feminist researchers who deal with it. There are feminists who argue that women's experiences and socialization, not their genes, lead them to have different ways of thinking, different conceptualization of problems. There are some studies that suggest that in groups, women leaders have different styles in group research. On the other hand, there are a large number of women who enter professions and adopt the same approaches in scientific research, education, etc. as male scientists. The values they adopt are those of the profession."

We reported almost all answers by respondents because of the difficulty we experienced in trying to pin down their position. They distance themselves from any biological account for different approaches to science by women, but they also believe that women all do science differently. Without being uncharitable, it appears that most respondents are expressing the *hope* that women will make a difference. Given the dissatisfaction with science expressed by feminists, they want to believe that they will be more concerned about human and animal subjects, that they will be less competitive, and that their styles will be more personal and involved, rather than objective. To have said otherwise, that is, women and men in physics will do the same kind of physics, would be to accept the existence of an approved body of theory and methods about which there is great consensus. Feminist respondents cannot say this, since they have already asserted the existence of male-dominated definitions of science.

Thus, the feminist respondents reveal considerable unease with science. Unhappy with science's exclusion of women as scientists and subjects, they do not see big effects following the influx of women in science. They clearly want women to be part of the institution of science at the same time they are actively trying to change science. But change to what is less clear.

POLITICS AND SCIENCE:
WHOEVER PAYS THE PIPER CALLS THE TUNE

There was a time, perhaps fifty years ago, when science was a relatively small-scale activity, conducted by individuals or small teams in small laboratories across a handful of universities and a small number of research hospitals and laboratories. World War II brought the age of Big Science, conducted by inter-related teams of scientists working on topics funded primarily by the federal government but also private funds. Has this shift to Big Science benefited society?

Four of the feminist respondents believe that Big Science was necessary for many of the major projects of the modern era (e.g., nuclear power) and for expanding the level of involvement of scientific research. Moreover, they feel that the results have been beneficial. The other five respondents question the value of the development of large research enterprises. One concern is that expensive projects "drain resources from small projects" and that "some of the fundamental work that should be done gets lost." Another concern is more explicit, in that it links Big Science with a certain kind of scientific work that is actually harmful.

- "Most government-supported scientific research has been directed toward the military. Some spin-off has been of some use outside of military. Only a small percent of funding has been directed to explicit human benefit. Even cancer research support, which has been high, has not changed the rate of women dying of cancer from what it was forty years ago. Overall, science has created more illness and not succeeded in being very effective. I don't think the figures on life expectancy and infant mortality have changed much in our country [in recent years]. Overall, I'm very skeptical that science has had a beneficial effect."

And how should scientific research be funded, regardless of the size of scientific projects? Does the federal government have a *responsibility* to fund scientific research? Should private funding be used for research in universities? Feminists are suspicious of both government and private funding, less suspicious of the former and very suspicious of the latter.

- "Government has a responsibility for the well-being of those it governs. I don't know if the research it funds benefits society. The important thing is to have diversity of science funding."
- "I think the government does [have such a responsibility], to a degree, but it has gotten out of hand. It is too big and influences too many other aspects of society, such as the university, in the wrong way."

Private funding, however, comes under the greatest criticism and the most suspicion. In this regard, feminist views reveal a greater affinity with the political left's criticism of corporations than with the right's criticism of government.

- "I think it's very dangerous. It's closely related to problems I see with scientists being associated with values of greed and power and prestige—because that's what corporations run on."
- "Private funding is problematic when it is the main source of funding. They get their fingers into the work and try to determine it. It's the same problem with the government."
- "If a company wants to do research, they should have their own scientists and not expect the university to carry out the work. They fund research that benefits them. The universities are acting as a research branch of a particular company."

Feminists discussion of how science is funded, whether by government or private corporations, suggests an image of "science corrupted" or "science captured." The resources and talents of scientists are turned in the direction of serving a political agenda (e.g., military projects) or a financial agenda (e.g., developing products for a market). Governmental and corporate agendas not only "distort" the research agenda, but they corrupt individual scientists.

SCIENCE AND RELIGION: GOD'S PLAN OR AN ALTERNATIVE PLAN?

The final subject of our interviews concerns the relationship between religion and science. We were interested in whether people see these two systems of thought as compatible or incompatible, and whether their balance of influence in society has changed in recent years. We were also interested in how people viewed the introduction of religious ideas in science courses and social studies courses at the pre-college and college levels of instruction. Writers who believe that science as an institution is under attack often identify one source of the attack as those who favor biblical creationism as an account of the human species on earth.

The controversy surrounding the role of religion in the school curriculum seems to have carried over to the feminist respondents. Their responses to questions about religion and science are more varied than for any of the other topics covered in the interviews. This is contrary to what might be expected, given the homogeneity of this group in terms of education (almost all Ph.D.s), employment (almost all professors or university administrators), or ideology (all are involved in feminist/women's organizations). This suggests that the issue cuts across traditional boundaries of group ties and identities.

Three respondents seem to take a traditional "separation of church and state" position. Science and religion are either incompatible, or at least incompatible with the conservative religions that make an issue of evolutionary theory or prayer in schools. They see no reason for introducing religion in science courses at any level.

- "I think religion belongs in theology courses."
- "Religious beliefs are very personal and they have nothing to do with teaching science. Religion cannot be used to filter the science that is taught. A course in comparative religion would be fine."
- "Science and religion are two different subjects. Those who support creationism are anti-science. The debate does not belong in the science classroom."

Three other respondents feel that religion and science are compatible and they identify circumstances under which it might be appropriate to include religion in courses.

- "For me, they have always been compatible. Nothing in science denies the existence of an omnipotent being, a higher being. There is nothing in the Bible about not doing science."

- "I tend to see them as separate explanatory domains. They are not necessarily incompatible, just separate."
- "I think they're compatible. I think you can be committed to an ethical life or some belief in a spiritual community and not have it undercut by scientific beliefs."

Let us now consider how these three respondents deal with teaching/curriculum issues.

Should professors have freedom to inject religion in college science courses?

- "A difficult question, because I believe in freedom of expression in the classroom. But I worry about authority figures who may present views contrary to the best knowledge. Maybe it would be better in a debate format. Students have to learn to deal with these issues."
- "Maybe religious views can be introduced at the beginning of the course, but not throughout the course."
- "I would never introduce religion unless it were really germane. You should not introduce your commitments, whether sexual orientation or religion, in the classroom. When you introduce your views it doesn't help the students."

Should professors have the freedom to inject religion into social studies courses?

- "I think you can because topics invite alternative perspectives on a subject. That is healthy, but its not an easy situation."
- "I can see how it might be relevant, but I am troubled by the introduction of faculty's religious beliefs. Are they relevant?"
- "Again, I don't think it's a good policy. Students figure out your personal views, but you have to encourage students to express different views and not to be preached to. I have disagreements with colleagues from time to time in women's studies about the extent to which you should push a particular feminist analysis. You can misuse your authority in the name of so many causes—religious ones, feminist ones, sexual freedom ones—in our classrooms."

Should both biblical creationism and Darwinian evolution be introduced in science courses in college?

- "I have difficulty seeing creationism as a scientific approach and therefore don't think it is relevant."
- "I favor presenting the scientific model. Creationism is not the only al-

ternative. Native Americans have their own views. I would favor a cross-cultural view—that might be the most interesting."

- "I would not be concerned if my children were only exposed to Darwinism. I think they would hear about creationism. I would have a hard time with a science teacher who introduces creationism."

Finally, there are two feminist respondents who see some religious beliefs as compatible with science and some as not compatible. Their views on the inclusion of religion in science courses are different from their colleagues'. They appear not to be endorsing religious beliefs, but are reluctant to take a position preventing their views from being presented in science and other classes. Perhaps their own experience in teaching potentially controversial subjects in women's studies makes them particularly sensitive to any kind of exclusion. They may fear that if today we exclude creationism, tomorrow it may be women's studies.

In any event, here is what they had to say.

Should professors have freedom to inject religion into college science courses?

- "They have it! They not only should have, but they have it. Nobody has taken away the right of teachers to introduce their religious beliefs into the classroom."
- "A very difficult question. I think we should be talking about values, beliefs, etc. I think religious beliefs do get into the classroom and I think we should fess up and make them explicit. The degree that those religious beliefs and values motivate a political agenda that tries to convert others into thinking and believing as I do—I think that's a problem. I don't know that the answer is to say, 'religion can't come in.' How we differentiate between someone who is trying to convert and someone who isn't, is a very difficult question to answer."

Should professors have freedom to inject religion into social studies courses?

- "They have every right to express their opinions. They do not have the right to exclude other opinions or perspectives. They don't have the right to say homosexuality is disgusting, a perversion, and forbidden by God and not allow somebody in the class or some text, or some other presentation."
- "It is inevitable that it is going to come in, and it's better that it's explicit than implicit. There needs to be a great deal of discussion with students about what is expertise, opinion, and desire. I may desire that my students think the way I think, but I should not act on that desire

in the classroom. I think there has to be frank and unambiguous disclosure by professors about why they feel the way they do on issues."

Should both biblical creationism and Darwinian evolution be introduced in science courses in college?

- "Neither is sufficient. They should not be presented side by side or as complementary stories. It's a no-win situation. I'm not satisfied with just teaching Darwinism and I'm not satisfied with just teaching creationism, and I'm not satisfied with teaching them side by side. Best thing to do is let the Supreme Court be the final arbiter. It's not a sufficient solution, but that's the only thing we can hope for."

LOCAL AND NATIONAL FEMINISTS

The feminist voice on science presents a wide range of concerns and criticisms about scientists and the institution of science. It would be inaccurate to characterize them as "anti-science" or "anti-reason," as they sometimes are characterized in the heat of debate about science. However, their criticisms are wide-ranging and deeply felt. Their views appear to be most unified when discussing the place of women in science, and in expressing their concerns about the control of scientific work by corporations or the government. They frequently distinguish between individual scientists and the institution of science, reserving their sharpest commentary for the latter. The feminist voice appears to be less unified and less forceful when discussing matters related to the environment and religion.

How do the views of these local feminist leaders compare to the more visible national feminist voices singled out by Gross and Levitt to represent the feminist position? Sandra Harding, for example, writing on the "Science Question in Feminism," points out that feminists have only recently turned their attention to the natural sciences.[3] According to Harding, the feminist effort to examine science has focused on five research programs. Let us examine each of these programs and how the local feminists have spoken to these issues.

(a) The first program involves documenting the historical barriers and continuing resistance to women's efforts to get the education, credentials, and jobs available to men. But once access is achieved, should women want to become "just like men" in science? "Should feminism set such a low goal as more equality with men," or should feminists be thinking about how to change the sexist, racist, and classist nature of science?

The local feminist leaders reveal extensive knowledge of the issues involved with this research program. They are aware of barriers that face women interested in science as a career, and are very articulate about the possibilities and limits for significant changes that might follow from greater involvement of women in science. Thus, on this research program the views of national and local feminists are quite similar.

(b) The second and third research programs are concerned with how science (especially biology) has engaged in sexist research. In discussing science's role in developing oppressive reproductive technologies, Harding raises the question of whether it is possible to speak of the proper uses of science to contrast with its improper uses. For Harding, this question concerns whether there can be "value-free pure scientific research." Although the problem of value-laden research is most apparent in biology, where the selection and definition of what is worth studying have been made by men, the issues extend to physics and chemistry as well.

The interviews with local feminist leaders reveal clear awareness and criticism of how male-dominated science has produced "bad science," that is, men's perception of problems are taken to be everyone's problems. However, these discussions do not lead to questions about whether science can be objective and value-free. Local feminists believe that women scientists may choose different subjects for study, and their research styles will be different (more personal and involved), but this does not lead to a discussion of whether science can be objective and value-free. This question does not appear to have the same salience for national (i.e., Harding) and local feminists.

(c) The fourth and fifth research programs of a feminist theory for the critique of the natural sciences are concerned with epistemological issues. The dominant modes of knowledge seeking in science, according to Harding, are "inextricably connected with specifically masculine—and perhaps uniquely Western and bourgeois—needs and desires. Objectivity vs. subjectivity, the scientist as knowing subject vs. the objects of his inquiry, reason vs. the emotions, mind vs. body—in each case the former has been associated with masculinity and the latter with femininity. In each case it has been claimed that human progress requires the former to achieve domination of the latter."[4]

Although the local feminists are undoubtedly aware of the issues surrounding the question of feminist epistemology as an alternative mode of knowledge seeking, such matters did not surface in the interviews. This may have been due to the type of questions posed, or simply that it was less important than the issue of increasing women's access to scientific careers.

Gross and Levitt choose to characterize the feminist critique of science mainly in terms of the third and fourth research programs described by Harding, namely, the epistemological critique. For example: "The new [feminist] criticism is far more sweeping: it claims to go to the heart of the methodological, conceptual, and epistemological foundations of science. It claims to provide a basis for a reformulation of science that reaches deeply into its context, its ideas, and its findings."[5]

Harding's first research program on the barriers and resistance to women's entry into, and full participation in, scientific careers is dismissed by Gross and Levitt. They choose to focus on the increasing participation of women in science, especially biomedical sciences, and view sexist discrimination as "largely vestigial."

Thus, what Gross and Levitt choose to focus on from Harding's critique of science is not what the local feminist leaders discuss when examining science. Local leaders are more concerned with practical, everyday-life issues flowing from a male-dominated science. They are concerned with the male bias in research topics and the exclusion of women from positions with the power to change scientific institutions. Abstract, theoretical questions about objectivity or a distinctively female science were not prominent subjects in the interviews with local feminists.

Reflections of an Environmentalist

"I think we're absolutely dependent upon scientists to get us out of this mess. I don't see how we can do it without them. But science will have to serve the goals of social justice and sustainability rather than the goal of profit."

I think I've always been interested in issues beyond the realm of my own personal life. Those issues have shifted over the years as they probably have for most people. It started out in anti-war work, affirmative action, Central American issues, opposition to our support for the Contras, and neighborhood organizing. I was an editor at a newspaper, and eventually, from a lot of information I was getting from the newspapers, my interests turned to the environment. I think acid rain was one of the first real issues that grabbed my attention. In the 1970s there was a lot of illegal dumping and serious environmental issues that had been brought to the public's attention for the first time. My degree was in English and I thought about going back to school to get a degree in environmental science. But I decided rather than putting the time and energy into getting a degree in science, I could do more good by jumping right in, educating myself, and becoming a community activist rather than a professional.

I think that my mother had some influence on me, not that she was politically active, but she was very active in hospital work. She managed all the volunteers for a hospital, and I remember, as a child, my mother being on the phone constantly. Although my personality is much less outgoing than my mother's, as an adult I find myself doing the same thing—-always on the phone getting people to do things. Now my children perceive me the same way that I perceived my mother.

John F. Kennedy's election had an effect on me. I was in the seventh or eighth grade, and since I was a Catholic growing up in Chicago, that was a big event in my family. We were a Democratic family in a mostly Republican area. The kind of idealism expressed in his "ask what you can do for your country," really affected me. I used that speech in a paper I did in the eighth grade. And then there was the civil rights movement and some of the teachers in the Catholic school had talked about their involvement.

I had a very strong religious education and went to a Catholic school through the eighth grade. I remember a final exam in the eighth grade that asked for the biblical and Christian justification for private property. And I was very upset because I was a good student, and I had absolutely no idea what the answer could be, and I still don't know. I'm not terribly religious today and haven't been as an adult. It was important in my formative years, but sometimes when I pick up the Bible now and read it, I'm shocked by what's in there. Still, I think that environmentalism seems consistent with the Christianity that I learned, although the connection is not necessarily strong.

I don't think that feminist issues were connected to my environmental activism. Feminism played more of a role in my personal life, my personal relationships, but it wasn't the basis for my activism. I can see how there might be a connection between feminism and environmentalism, especially when you get into health issues, but I haven't thought too much about that connection.

I came to environmentalism from a political stance, from looking at capitalism, industrialization, and corporate America rather than looking at male-dominance issues. I look at our society through a political paradigm, so I look at corporations, who is in control, and who makes the decisions. There could be a link here to feminism, because the people in corporations who are making decisions about illegal dumping or health issues are often men.

We need to build a society where the emphasis is on sustainability, where there is more hope for the future—a society where concern for the future is built into the decisions that we make, rather than the one we now have, which seems to be built on consumption and profit. We also need to be a fairer society, without the huge differences between those with millions and billions and other people who don't have enough to eat. In my ideal society, there would be environmental, political, and economic justice.

Science has a role to play in building a more just society, especially in the environmental area. I'd like to see scientists helping farmers who are trying to use fewer chemicals, but don't always have a lot of sound information about how to do it. The land-grant universities should be field-testing organic farming methods and working on solar energy and wind power. The problem is that these are political decisions, and scientists have to get the resources to do that kind of work. A lot of research is paid for directly by corporations, so a lot of science is under corporate direction. On the other hand, there is a lot of science funded by the government, even though we seem to wind up in the same place. At least there is more hope that federally and state funded science has the potential to be beneficial to the environment, compared to science funded by corporations.

There are some research and some technological developments that should not be supported. An example that is more technology than science is our ability to over-fish, to harvest so many fish that we are threatening the food supply. Then there is all the research on anti-bacterials that has led to products like baby toys with anti-bacterial components. This is done without a thought to environmental consequences, only trying to sell more products. So on the one hand, you have industry cranking out anti-bacterial products, and on the other hand mainstream health newsletters are advising people not to use them. These two examples show that the idea behind the research or technology is selling more products, whether fish or anti-bacterial toys. An economy that is based so heavily on consumption, as ours is, cannot be sustainable. How can we conserve resources when the key thing is to keep the economic machine running by consumption? The globalization of the economy only adds to our problems. The idea of buying apples from New Zealand and using fossil fuel to ship them here, or exporting rice to Japan, shows what a strong tie there is between our economic system and environmental problems. There should be more emphasis on localism and regionalism in our economic production and distribution.

It seems to me that the general public today is less optimistic about science and more skeptical or cynical or cautious than they used to be. Some of this is due to the big new projects, like human genome research, that have generated conflicting views. Some people see the possibility that dreaded diseases will be eliminated as a result of genetic research, but for others it opens up areas that make them uncomfortable, like genetically altered agricultural products. There is less concern here than in Europe, where it's a major environmental issue.

I don't agree with those who criticize environmentalists for being fear-mongers. I think that the environmental movement developed just in the nick of time. If we had continued going the way we were, with no environmental protections and toxic dumping and nuclear energy growing, I don't want to think of what the environment would be like today. What the experts told us about the safety of DDT and the safety of pesticides absolutely had to be questioned. Even if the movement sometimes exaggerates potential problems and it looks like fear-mongering, I'm willing to accept that as the price I'm willing to pay for more environmental protection. It's not a tactic I agree with, and it's a long-term struggle to keep these things from tainting the movement.

I see great potential for scientists to work together with environmentalists. I think scientists have been hesitant to take a position on environmental problems. It's sometimes frustrating that we can't always get support from scientists. Scientists are always so careful in what they say, that to take a position on an issue is sometimes difficult. But there are scientists who have done that, and I can see, given the nature of human knowledge and how it develops, something that's true today isn't always true tomorrow. I can understand how scientists hesitate sometimes about taking a stand. But I do think that it would be necessary in the future for scientists to take a stand on issues, and maybe by doing that they can redirect science into areas that are important for our society.

Chapter 3

Environmentalists and the Control of Nature

The image of spaceship Earth as a tiny blue and white marble floating alone in a vast open space provides a compelling metaphor for the inter-relation and inter-dependence of all living things on Earth. Ultimately, the possibilities of living together or dying together on this tiny planet depend on how humans view the ecosystem, and what it requires for survival. This image of spaceship Earth is a product of ecological science and is accepted by both the defenders and critics of science's environmental consciousness. Gross and Levitt, for example, are quick to acknowledge the delicate balance between the size of the earth's population, the structure of its ecosystem, and its environmental carrying capacity. The earth's carrying capacity has limits, and "technology cannot forever transcend carrying capacity."[1] Carolyn Merchant, an ecologist who is very critical of science, also views the ecological crisis in terms of the balance between contradictory forces involved in production, reproduction, and ecology. She writes that "the [ecological] crisis could be relieved over the next several decades, however, through a global ecological revolution brought about by changes in production, reproduction, and consciousness that lead to ecological sustainability."[2]

Despite their apparent acceptance of an ecosystem model of the earth, defenders and critics of science appear to part company when discussing the responsibility of science and scientists for existing environmental problems and when considering what science can do to provide remedies. The radical environmentalist Jeremy Rifkin believes that most of our problems concerning science and the environment are rooted in the way we think about scientific knowledge. We tend to think about knowledge as power, and thus "our interest is always focused on knowing how things manifest themselves so that we can use, exploit, harness and control them."[3] Rifkin claims that the proponents of this kind of "controlling knowledge" have brought us to the brink of extinction with such "achievements" as the nuclear bomb and genetic engineering. Rifkin calls for replacing controlling knowledge with empathic knowledge that will help us to connect with nature rather than control it, and offers a glimpse of how an empathetic approach might work in engineering, physics, and medicine. The central point of Rifkin's critique is that the old approach of controlling knowledge can only compound our problems, and a new approach is needed: "The fact of the matter is that we have reached the end of the line for a method of human inquiry that has accompanied us from the first day of our journey into human consciousness. . . . Though we are actually reluctant to part with a way of thinking that has been, for so long, the defining characteristic of the species, it is becoming painfully evident that any further reliance on this form of knowledge would be self-defeating for the human race."[4]

The most ardent defenders of science, such as Gross and Levitt, are inclined to dismiss what they call the "apocalyptic naturism" that relies on inflated language and political tactics designed to induce panic and an immediate restructuring of society. They prefer to rely on the research of ecological scientists to do the comprehensive studies that will guide environmental policies, thereby preserving the authority of science. Gross and Levitt view radical environmentalists such as Merchant and Rifkin as "unwilling or bitterly reluctant to accept scientific work that confutes or modifies alarmist theories."[5]

How are these sharp differences between defenders and critics of science reflected in the views of rank-and-file environmentalists, those persons who hold positions of leadership in local chapters of environmental organizations?

When asked whether science has made life better or worse in their lifetime, only a minority of respondents were unequivocal in saying "yes," pointing to advances in medicine, computers, and chemistry. The majority, however, felt it necessary to indicate both the "better" and the "worse," or to say that science has made "life different" but "I'm not quite sure it's made it better." Two of those expressing equivocal views are very specific about science having been worse for the environment.

- "Sometimes I think that science has made us less appreciative of our environment. We are more interested in knowing how we can control things rather than allowing them to be."
- "There have been advances in medical science and some problems such as environmental contamination."

This equivocal view of the benefits of science appears to carry over to the degree of confidence in what scientists say to the public on matters of nutrition and health, pesticides, and nuclear energy. Again, a majority offer qualifications to their level of confidence that sound like the kind of skepticism often associated with a scientific attitude.

- "Yes, I have confidence in general, but there are so many ways to look at an issue. I have less trust that just the science perspective is enough."
- "The older I get, the more skeptical I am of the information I get. There are fewer scientific certainties than I once thought. The scientific certainties are temporary."

The cautious and qualified responses to questions about the benefits of science or their confidence in science do not appear to be related to the fact that scientists often disagree about questions of global warming or nuclear energy. All but one of our respondents view disagreements among scientists to be a healthy, normal feature of science. As one respondent put it: "Scientists are only working with models, and they are incomplete. They don't have all the data. I don't find disagreement strange or disconcerting. That's the nature of science."

Although it is often said that public disagreement among scientists tends to turn off the general public from listening to anyone or from being interested in science-related public issues, this is not the case for our respondents. Acceptance of disagreement is undoubtedly related to our respondents' background in science education and, in some cases, their work as biologists or chemists. The awareness of disagreement among scientists appears to induce many of our interviewees to become more involved in sorting out the reasons for the differing views.

- "I look for some kind of consensus in the scientific community, and I also look for scientists' other relationships, like who is funding their work."
- "We subscribe to *Nature,* my husband is a member of the American Chemical Society, and we recognize certain researchers who have more credibility than others—the ones who don't go overboard and do careful work."
- "As a scientist I expect these debates to go on, and from my perspective I just want to know what the weight of the evidence is. I tend to be swayed by the consensus and/or the data."

Perhaps what is most noteworthy about the local environmentalists' views of science expressed above is the fact that, although cautious in their views of science, they remain wedded to science as a valid way of studying the natural world. Nothing that has been said would appear to resonate with the views of the radical environmentalists presented at the beginning of this chapter.

Let us now turn to questions of misconduct among scientists and scientists' ethical standards. When asked if they consider most scientists to be sensitive to the ethical implications of their work, a majority of environmentalists express doubts. Some express doubts about "most," feeling that some scientists are sensitive to ethical issues, but not most scientists. Regardless of differences over whether they are talking about some or most scientists, this majority of environmentalists uniformly believe that scientists will proceed with their research agendas despite any particular awareness or sensitivity to ethical issues.

- "I would not say most are concerned with ethical issues. They have other agendas—advancing their career, getting grant money."
- "Yes, some are sensitive to issues, but whether or not they feel that science should go on is another matter."
- "I used to do DNA research and people in the lab would make jokes about the concerns of people. There is a lot of ego in research, and they are not respectful of the beliefs of average people. Most scientists are aware of ethical issues but they don't focus on them. It's a conflict of interest."
- "Most? I think many are but not most. They get so tied up in what they're doing, they don't think long term. Part of it's financial, because their job and money depends on more research."

All but one of the environmentalists were able to discuss in some detail cases of misconduct by scientists, such as falsification of data. The reasons given for such misconduct include the familiar list of suspects. "Greed. People who are more interested in their own gain over anything else," said one respondent. Another focused on the arrogance and self-absorption of scientists: "It's probably more ambition and a kind of arrogance by someone who believes so strongly that he is right that he doesn't have to bother with the accuracy of all the data." Almost all mentioned the pressures of publishing and getting research funds as directly or indirectly responsible for most cases of misconduct.

We now turn to how the environmentalists view the activities of science in relation to four specific areas: the environment, women, politics, and religion. Keep in mind that we are interested in the nature and extent of criticism leveled at science across the four subject areas, and whether the concerns that are expressed are most serious or intensive when discussing the environment.

NATURE, SCIENCE, AND CITIZENS: WHAT IS THE BALANCE?

The environmentalist respondents were given an opportunity to discuss the relation between science and nature as it bears on the matter of science as a means to control nature. They appear to be equally divided on this issue, with half discussing the matter in terms similar to Rifkin's contrast between controlling knowledge and empathic knowledge.

- "I'm a basic scientist and I think we should know how the world works. We, as humans, are only a small part of how the whole thing works, and it's detrimental to be anthropocentric about the use of science."
- "We need to learn about how our world works, but not to take that information solely to control the workings of our world. Scientists shouldn't singularly have control over how knowledge is used."
- "Now, you're talking to a geologist who is very upset about man's modifying nature. It seems that every time we start messing around with Mother Nature, we get into more trouble than we've been in before."
- "We should learn about nature first. When we apply it, it should be to help all species, not just man."

In contrast, the other half of environmentalists do not seem troubled by an "active" science that has application of knowledge as a goal. At the very least, they believe that society benefits from both basic research and the application of that knowledge for human purposes. However, when they discuss application they seem to be thinking of the planet as well as humans. Consider the following comment.

- "The prime goal should not be pure research, in any direction, but research that somehow improves the human lot in a large sense, by improving the health of the planet. The fate of humankind and the earth should be the goal of science."

This view of how scientific knowledge could be used to improve the environment is revealed more explicitly by respondents expressing concern about the need for more involvement by scientists with citizens working together to shape public policy. We asked environmentalists about their opinion of whether scientists or citizens should provide the leadership on environmental issues. Two spoke directly to the question of participation by scientists.

- "I usually find myself working with citizens, and truthfully I wish that more scientists were involved. I don't know many scientists who are working on environmental issues, but those who are, are a powerful force. There should be more, especially in the area of toxics. The decision makers should be citizens working with scientists who provide the information that is needed."

- "I wish scientists would do more. Scientists are reluctant to speak, and are discouraged from speaking unless they have the statistical evidence. I would like to see them be the leaders because they have the social respect. Citizens don't carry the clout [I do] when I go to an Audubon meeting."

All the environmentalists stressed the need for both scientists and citizens to be involved, but they tended to discuss the citizens as being *on top* (the decision makers), while the scientists are *on tap* (providing the information). This division of labor may reflect our respondents' beliefs about what scientists and citizens do best. But there is also a touch of suspicion about how far you can expect science to go in the struggle to clean up the environment. This suspicion is reflected in the above environmentalist quote which states that scientists won't speak unless they have the facts. It is also reflected in the following remarks.

- "The problem with scientists is that they tend to be apolitical. Citizens have a role because they can be involved politically. But the information must come from scientists."
- "I really think it needs to be both, because lots of people will want to know the scientific facts. There are also lots of people who are skeptical enough about having just science."

The criticism of science by environmentalists does not appear to have quite the content of the radical environmentalists who are seeking to replace scientific knowledge and authority with a different approach to environmental issues. The environmentalists interviewed in this study continue to rely on the utility of science for dealing with the environment at the same time that they are cautious or skeptical about expecting too much from the scientific community. They welcome greater participation by scientists in environmental movements, but they are not prepared to accept them as leaders. There appears to be a preference for citizen leadership combined with the expertise of scientists, because the latter are viewed as less able or willing to enter into political battles.

A final question posed to our environmentalists concerned their views of "radical" or "gradual" approaches to environmental problems. The former refers to limitations in energy consumption and pesticide use, while the latter involves recycling and voluntary lifestyle change. Our respondents are clearly realists in their approach to change, something that they have learned in their leadership roles in local environmental organizations. Although not opposed to radical change, they universally repeat phrases like

"Anything too radical is not going to be accepted" or "You are not going to get changes in auto transportation unless you have mass transportation." In general, they try to indicate that all efforts are needed as long as they continue to increase people's sensitivity to the need for changing the way we use energy, consume, and discard products.

WOMEN AND SCIENCE: PAST, PRESENT, AND FUTURE

Environmentalists were presented with the statement that, historically, science has been a male-dominated enterprise, and they were asked to discuss how this may have influenced science. The responses to this query, in terms of detail provided and the ease of response, suggest that this is not a hot-button item for most environmentalists. Three of the respondents did provide the automatic response of "well, of course" and proceeded to mention the inattention to women's diseases in medical science. These responses were similar in tone and content to those offered by all the feminist respondents. But the majority of the environmentalists provided rather low-key responses that would suggest that the subject of women and science does not have high salience for them.

- "I don't think so. Maybe there is less cooperativeness in the way that men work."
- "In chemistry I don't think it has mattered. In geology it doesn't make much difference, either. It's made a difference in the medical area."
- "Yes. There are certain emotional or creative differences between men and women."
- "Of course, dime-store psychology tells you rockets are more male. I'm sure it has [made a difference] but I can't say exactly in what ways."
- "Sure, but I can't give any examples off the top of my head."

The environmentalists did not exhibit high optimism regarding what one might expect to occur from the recent increased participation of women in science. Although they will acknowledge that there may be some difference in choice of research topics, especially with regard to women's health issues, they seem to believe that little change should be expected. For example:

- "Other than the inclusion of women's diseases and things like that, I think that women scientists are interested in the same things as male scientists. They are scientists! So I don't see the choice of topic being tremendously different in most areas."
- "I haven't been able to discern [any difference] yet. Maybe in medicine with more women doctors, there will be more research done on medical

conditions that primarily affect women. I don't see any effects in chemistry or physics."
- "A lot of science now has been making things that are consumer oriented, but they don't contribute to survival or a quality of life effect. I don't know if women will change this because of the funding. There will be a slightly different viewpoint, but the women are going to have the same aims as the men—job security, financial security for families."

We believe that the responses by environmentalists to the questions about women and science are far more subdued and less optimistic than those offered by feminists. The latter were more critical of science for the historical exclusion of women, and more optimistic about what might result from the infusion of more women in science. This difference between environmentalists and feminists is also revealed when examining the environmentalists responses to the question of whether women scientists will do science differently than their male colleagues. Only one environmentalist believes they will do science differently than men, but the response is very general: "I suspect there will be [a difference] but I don't know if I can put my finger on it." The rest of the environmentalists do not believe that women will conduct scientific work in a way different from men. A typical response follows.

- "I haven't seen any indications of that. I haven't seen any feminist methodology that differs from prevailing methods of experimentation and replication—at least from what my daughter is learning in science courses."

In summary, the views of environmentalists concerning the role of women in science do not exhibit much in the way of intense feelings and may best be summed up in the words of one respondent, who said, "I guess I'm more of an environmentalist than a feminist."

POLITICS AND SCIENCE:
WHOEVER PAYS THE PIPER CALLS THE TUNE

We now examine how environmentalists feel about the post–World War II era of Big Science, characterized by the need for extensive funds for research from the federal government, private foundations, and corporations. Respondents were presented with the following statement for their reaction: "Before World War II most science was done by individual scientists working in small laboratories. Today, much science is done by government-funded teams of scientists using complex and expensive tools. Overall, would you say that this change has or has not benefited society?"

Only one respondent provided a clear statement that society has not benefited from Big Science. Another is also negative, but not as clearly or strongly.

- "Well, we start with the atom bomb, which was one of the first big projects. That's a tough question. I don't think I can say that it has benefited society when I think of atomic energy, high chemical input into farming. I'm not against government spending, but it has not been used in a positive way."
- "I don't know. It's probably done harm. The drawback of government spending is control over what is done. But then, it's better to have government funding than industrial funding."

The remaining majority of environmentalists believe that society has benefited from Big Science. They recognize that funding provides the opportunity to work on important topics and to develop the complicated equipment needed in such research. As one respondent put it, "There is probably very little that can be done today by a person working alone, except for mathematicians and theoretical physicists. But even they need expensive computers."

Amid the positive statements about the benefits of Big Science, there were some concerns over whether "Big Science inhibits diversity and creativity" and whether it leads to efforts to produce results quickly. As one person stated, "What should be a ten-year study of the effects of some drug becomes a five-year study, with questionable results."

The environmentalists are quite enthusiastic in believing that the federal government has a responsibility to fund scientific research. Their comments are a marked contrast with the suspicious tone of the responses of feminists and the political left and right.

- "The federal government is us. As a society we have to decide what we want to do with our money and look at the consequences of that. If we decide to attack cancer, we have to put our taxes into that and the government has to divvy up the money. If we don't want taxes, then we are probably not going to have cures for cancer or space exploration."
- "If you think science is to serve the people for the betterment of life, then the government has a responsibility to fund research. And for the kind of things that would be for the general welfare, it would be very hard to get money from a company that has financial interests."
- "Yes, definitely. I think the government, through its spending practices, has to reward scientists who will benefit the society. They need to fund alternatives to pesticides and support farming practices that will not require pesticides."

- "Yes, because scientific research is needed to remain globally competitive. The government may be able to provide more neutral funding than industry, which is totally profit driven. And I think the government is there to solve social problems."

When asked how they feel about private corporations providing funding for university research, the environmentalists' responses are more varied and less enthusiastic. Three environmentalists see no problem with private corporations funding university research.

- "That's fine. They usually have a goal in mind when they fund a specific line of research, and I don't see anything wrong with that. They can fund a university or they can fund within the framework of their own corporation."
- "That's the way a lot of research gets done. Research has become very expensive. It's the instruments that are very costly. I see no problem with private funding."
- "Sounds fine. I don't see any reason why not."

At the other extreme are two environmentalists who have reservations about private funding of university research.

- "I'm very skeptical of that. As an environmentalist, if someone says there are no problems with the groundwater and their research has been funded by Eli Lilly—well, I take that with a grain of salt. [I] wouldn't automatically discount research funded by private corporations, but I am more skeptical. Obviously, corporations have a vested interest in the results."
- "It can be very biased, as in the agro-chemical industry's pushing agricultural research along profit lines for years. There is nothing wrong with them making a contribution, but it should be balanced with alternative directions and sources of funding."

The remaining environmentalists seem to provide a cautious, tentative endorsement of private funding.
- "I think it's fine. It can be a problem when faculty become grant oriented they will slant their research."
- "I think it's important. The only downside is if those monies dictate the kind of questions that are asked. That would be detrimental."
- "Theoretically it's fine, but there is always an ethics problem. The motivation behind corporate support can influence outcomes."

In general, the environmentalists interviewed in this study are not especially troubled by Big Science and its consequences for society. They view government funding for research as both essential and beneficial. They have some concern about private corporation funding of university research, but they are not nearly as concerned or suspicious as were the feminist respondents. This difference in response to private-sector funding is probably linked to environmentalists' educational and career backgrounds in science and their greater exposure to the practice of corporate funding.

SCIENCE AND RELIGION

The final section of our interviews was concerned with the relationship between science and religion. The questions posed to our respondents were in three areas: (1) Are religious beliefs and scientific beliefs compatible or incompatible? (2) Has the relationship between science and religion changed in the last generation? (3) How do you feel about the introduction of religious opinions and beliefs by professors and teachers in college, high school, and elementary school?

On the first question, the overwhelming majority of environmentalists personally believe that science and religion are compatible, although they recognize that some religions might not agree. Thus, they recognize and acknowledge the existence of opposition to science from some segments of the religious community, but they do not associate themselves with such views. Here is what they have to say.

- "Depends on how you define religious beliefs. I consider myself a religious person and I find them compatible. I don't feel myself constrained by religion. I guess you're going to get conflict with fundamentalists who believe that the world was created in seven days. Many scientists I know are religious and show wonder and awe at the creation of the universe. I think the more you know, the more you realize what a fantastic universe we have."
- "It depends on how you define religion. They're compatible because they are mutually exclusive. Some religious fanatics have blurred the distinction."
- "I think beliefs are compatible in general, but not for specific beliefs in specific religions."
- "There are many religions that are extremely hostile toward science. I think ultimately they would all be very compatible."
- "I think they're compatible, but it possibly depends on what those religious beliefs are. I was raised as a Catholic, and people who taught me didn't seem to have a problem with Darwinian evolution."

Those environmentalists who feel that science and religion are incompatible seem to take the position that their core beliefs cannot be reconciled.

- "From what I've seen, for some people it's completely incompatible. In geology you run across people who believe that the world was created in 6000 B.C. on a certain day. This upsets everything in terms of the fossil record. . . . It depends on how you interpret the Bible. If you take it literally, word for word, you are in big trouble. You can't reconcile science and the Bible."
- "They are two different things. One is faith and the other is fact."

The two environmentalists who believe that religion and science are incompatible tend to feel that the balance of influence in society has today shifted to religion.

- "The creationists have become more vocal and influential. Right here in this county they are in the process of taking over the Republican party. It's scary, trying to take the teaching of evolution out of the schools."
- "Religion is more important today than earlier."

Several of the environmentalists who believe that religion and science are compatible tend to be concerned about the rise of the religious conservative movement, but they are less certain about whether a definite shift of influence to religion has occurred. However, most environmentalists believe that science is more influential in society today. Several expressed the following views.

- "I think science is a more important force in people's lives today, whether or not they realize it. People look to science for answers to problems more and more. Religion is a personal belief system, but it is not going to put down pesticide use, or clean up a river, or see that we have an adequate food supply."
- "There was a time when religion told science what it could and couldn't do. In fact there are some religious groups that still try to do that. Science has broken out of those shackles and is not concerned about religious authority determining what it can and can't do."
- "Definitely I think it's changing increasingly because scientific knowledge has really developed, and religious folks are going to have to adapt to this knowledge."

Questions about the place of religion in schools result in a variety of interesting and intensely felt responses. When discussing the possible introduction of creation science into the science curriculum in high school or college, environmentalists are unanimously opposed without qualification.

- "If you're asking should a professor introduce creation science, I would say absolutely not. Philosophically, creation science requires you to shut your brain off and I'm dead set against that."
- "If it's a biology course, it should present biology. Creationism has not been accepted by the biology community as scientific. Creationism belongs in a philosophy or theology course, not in biology."

The environmentalists' opposition to the inclusion of creationism in the science curriculum is undoubtedly related to their backgrounds as science students and professionals. They recognize the value of students being informed about creationism, but not in science courses. Several commented as follows.

- "At some point people need to know that what they are learning [Darwinian evolution] is not accepted by others in society, but I don't think creationism should be taught as an alternative."
- "It should be part of the educational experience, but I have no idea how or when."
- "Creationism is a historical view based on less knowledge. If it could be presented as historical views and then Darwin came along and developed his view, that would probably be fine. I have a problem if it [creationism] is not put in that perspective."

Environmentalists are more willing to allow a religious perspective to be included in college courses dealing with human sexuality, family planning, or health. They recognize that religion and morality are culturally shaped and are of relevance when dealing with human sexuality. However, they remain troubled about the role of religion in non-science courses in elementary and high school, citing such things as the maturity of students and the role of parents in providing values education. Finally, the environmentalists have different opinions on how much freedom professors should have to introduce their religious opinions in any class in college.

- "That's a touchy issue. If they're simply going to express an opinion, that's fine. If there's any kind of coercion to get students to endorse that opinion, I draw the line there. When I was in college students and professors had more interaction outside the classroom, and religion was always a topic. That's a much better place for such discussions."
- "Professors should have freedom for opening discussion of many faiths, but not only their faith or perspective. Then it's indoctrination. If they can keep the discussion multifaceted it's okay."
- "If they interject their opinion and say it's their opinion, okay. I don't like it, but they should have that freedom."

- "I don't think so. Professors have a strong hold on shaping opinions of students and this [interjecting their religious opinions] might lead to misuse of that influence."
- "I know of a chemistry professor who started off his course this fall with a prayer which ended in Jesus' name, with no thought for any other religious beliefs in the class. That's a no-no. I think he should keep his personal opinions to himself."

It is interesting that environmentalists are more uniformly opposed to the introduction of religion into science courses than are the feminists discussed in chapter 2. This may be linked to disciplinary experiences, as the environmentalists are rooted in the life sciences while the feminists are drawn from the social sciences and humanities. Creation science as part of the college curriculum might pose more of a threat to the way of thinking of environmentalists than it does to feminists. On the other hand, creation science has an affinity with religious fundamentalists whose views on abortion, the traditional family, and multiculturalism should be contrary to feminist beliefs. Thus, the *strong* opposition of environmentalists to the introduction of religion in schools is understandable, but the *lukewarm* opposition of feminists is not. As we speculated in the chapter on feminists, it may be related to being in marginalized fields in academe (e.g., women's studies) that they are reluctant to exclude others even when the others are ideological opponents.

In the final analysis, how can we locate the views of the local environmental leaders relative to those of national leaders who are critical of science, and of Gross and Levitt, who are critical of radical environmentalists such as Carolyn Merchant and Jeremy Rifkin? The views of Merchant that are selected for discussion by Gross and Levitt cover several points. First is the vision of "apocalyptic naturism," that ecological problems are of such magnitude that their resolution "is possible only through revolutionary reconstruction of society" such as a "reversion to edenic simplicity."[6] Second, have science and capitalism "desacralized nature, leaving it prey to the rapacity of technological capitalism"?

This characterization of Merchant's position fails to acknowledge her description of several variants of radical ecology. There are "social ecologists," who combine scientifically based ecological principles with a homocentric approach. Then there are the "deep ecologists," some of whom "wish to focus on redefining the meaning of self, others on redefining science and cosmology, still others on the connection between spirituality and deep ecology."[7] Then there are the eco-feminists, who stress the socially constructed nature of science (and of gender), the need for gender equality, and the necessity of subordinating production to an ethic of nurturing both humans and nature. Merchant recognizes that radical ecology lacks coherence as a theory and as a movement, but Gross and Levitt do not acknowledge the several variants of radical ecology and the deep divisions among them.

The local environmental leaders in this chapter are clearly social ecologists with deep roots in science. They would not recognize themselves in Gross and Levitt's description of radical environmentalists.

Reflections from the Political Right

"We are way past the Club of Rome's predictions of doom and gloom. We are still able to feed the world. People are going hungry, but not because the earth does not produce the food. It's a distribution problem."

Science is just one of the many things we deal with in life. I have faith in the scientific method because of my belief in repeatability of the natural order. And that natural order is an aspect of God's creation. God is a faithful God and He sees to it that the natural order always works and that the phenomena of the natural order will continue to be repeatable.

I became a Christian in college. Gave my life to Christ. And it's my faith in God that gives me faith in science and technology. If I could look at the owner's manual of the creation of the universe, I would see that things actually make sense and actually work. My training is in the hard sciences, particularly computer science, but also physics, chemistry, and biology. I see in the repeatability of these sciences the handiwork of God.

Because of these beliefs, I don't place any limits on what science should investigate as it seeks knowledge of the world around us. I see parallels between the natural laws that science can discover and moral laws. Both were made by the same God, and it would be very inconsistent for God to make two disparate kinds of laws. I see no incompatibility between the natural order and the moral order. On the other hand, are there particular kinds of research that should not be conducted? Yes! The Nazi experiments on the Jews! Simply put, good science can correct bad theology and good theology can correct bad science. Therefore, there can be no conflict between good science and good theology.

If we're talking about the potential in scientific and technological research to do damage, sure, it's there. But any knowledge can be used for good or for evil. No purely material object is either good or evil. No information, by itself, is either good or evil. Of course, in an ideal society, knowledge would be used only for good. My view of that ideal society is one where everybody would follow the commands of Jesus to love the Lord with all your heart, all your mind, all your strength, and all your soul. To love your neighbor as yourself and seek first the kingdom of God. But beyond that, social planning shouldn't impose a particular vision or model of society on everyone. There's no reason that you can't have a large diversity of models of society.

Science in itself certainly poses no threat to our society. Science and technology can make people's lives much easier. The question is not so much what tools are available as what people do with these tools. Of course, the source of sponsorship and support for scientific research does make a difference. When it comes to ethics, scientists are pretty much like everyone else: Some are ethical, some not. And maybe the focus on gaining new knowledge can blunt the ethical sense. That's why, in general, scientific research should not be supported by the government. The nature of the government is to follow the currently accepted line. It will tend to ignore or repress the real innovator—the maker of new paradigms—and will not reward the good scientist who happens to lack grantsmanship skills. And in principle, government has no responsibility or authority to fund any scientific or technological research except that related to national defense. I support the end of government funding of research just as I support the ending of all socialist programs. In advocating this, I, as a scientist, might personally suffer. My ox might be gored. But my personal interest doesn't affect the principle that's involved.

On the other hand, I do support corporate funding of research. This is the way it ought to be. Corporations live in the real world. Academics have been pretty isolated from the real world, and it's important that corporate realism determines what kind of research gets support.

Since God gave people stewardship of the earth, I would consider myself a conservationist rather than an environmentalist. The Lord placed Adam in a garden, not a pristine wilderness. And a garden is something you tend, take care of, cultivate, control. We should take care of the earth entrusted to us. But I don't see man as any contaminator of the earth. Sure, we'll make a little mistake here and there—even wipe out a little species—but that's no ecological disaster. God created a resilient system as a home for man.

Science is helpful. It will solve some significant problems, but it's not going to solve all our problems or give us a better society. That's because man is a spiritual being, and material gains don't meet all man's needs. We all have spiritual as well as material needs, and trying to meet spiritual needs with material things is like putting water in a car's gas tank instead of its radiator. The car needs water, but not in its gas tank.

It's for all these reasons that, when I'm pessimistic, it's a short-term pessimism. In the long run, I'm very much an optimist, because God will build His kingdom, and not just on this earth but beyond.

Science, to be effective, can and does use many ways to seek the truth and gain knowledge. Scientists don't all see things alike and think alike.

Take the idea of a revelation of knowledge, for instance. A revelation can be like a sudden and intuitive insight. Some people simply would not investigate such an insight further. But a disciplined scientist—a mathematician, for instance—will go ahead and test such an insight against standard methods of proof. Likewise, all of us gain knowledge by staying within a tradition of knowledge and accepting its authority, because we don't have the time to examine and test every bit of knowledge within this knowledge tradition. We continue to accept acknowledged authorities and accepted traditions. Only if something looks fishy will we investigate it more thoroughly. But realistically, if a certain authority has been reliable in the past, we tend to respect it.

Of course, needless to say, reason, observation, and experimentation are standard methods of obtaining knowledge. And not just in the realm of science. Honest scientists try to check all information sources, be they revelation, tradition, or authority, and try to verify them with reason, observation, and experiment. But there's no method of gaining knowledge that's unique to science.

In the final analysis, regardless of its source, something's either true or it's not. If it's true, it's true. If it's not, it's not.

Chapter 4

Political Right and Science Captured

Although political conservatives have not been as widely identified as enemies of science by defenders of science as have "the academic left" and "radical feminists and environmentalists," some pro-science warriors *have* characterized the irrationalism of the right as "far more nasty and virulent" and "in the final analysis, . . . much more powerful in the public arena" than the attacks of the left.[1]

Our sampling of the opinions of a group of political conservatives yields a picture of substantial surface support for and endorsement of science, and especially science-related technology, but it does show significant signs of mistrust. This mistrust seems to be directed more at scientists than at science as an institution, and focuses on scientists as potentially manipulable by other objects of suspicion, namely, the government and bureaucrats. Some of our respondents are especially wary of environmental scientists and express concern about the dogmatism of evolutionists.

The group of conservatives is unanimous in declaring that science has made life "easier and better," "much better," and "much, much better" than it was in earlier times. The object of their praise, however, like that of most of our groups of respondents, is not so much science as it is technology and technology-related science. It is these, rather than basic science, that are viewed as the principal engines of improvement; medical and agricultural research are singled out, for approbation, as are such technologies as cars, planes, and the new instruments of communication and information exchange. What seems missing is a sense of the historical and contemporary distinctions between science and technology, probably because of the apparent convergence of the two in recent years. Only one respondent in this group notes that a price has been exacted for the advantages conferred by science and technology. That price is identified as the inevitable governmental regulation and control that accompany technological change and that deprive the people of its full benefits.

Widespread belief that science and technology are responsible for a better life is not, however, reflected in high confidence in the information and judgments provided by scientists. A repeated theme is that scientists are human beings before they are scientists, and that they are subject to the same self-serving motives as everyone else. The subjectivity and dogmatism of some scientists are identified as further grounds for suspicion. Again, it is environmental scientists who are especially noted as unreliable sources of information. What these respondents characterize as the "junk science" of some environmentalists appears to conflict with the less highly controlled and more freewheeling and entrepreneurial approach to solving the problems of the environment and to the use of resources thought of as characteristic of political and economic conservatives.

This group shares the view of most of our respondents on the issue of public disagreements among scientists on matters of scientific fact or inference. These disagreements are quite easily accepted and tolerated by a number of our repondents. They say that "disagreement is part of the nature of science," that "disagreement is good; it is a stimulus for further thought," and that "disagreement is helpful as long as the competing opinions reflect an honest search for the truth and an absence of dogmatism." One respondent is supportive of such public disagreement because it puts responsibility on the individual to investigate and to resolve these differences by taking such steps as reading the literature and checking references. Others view all human behavior, including that of scientists, as ultimately political and hence biased. One respondent believes that many scientists, and especially environmental scientists, have political agendas and should have their comments ignored unless a check of their backgrounds indicates they are people of "moral integrity."

A very mixed response is elicited by the paired questions: Have the results of scientific research tended to support or reinforce beliefs or values you were brought up to accept? and Have the results of scientific research tended to challenge or threaten any beliefs or values you were brought up to accept? A few respondents implicitly distinguish between substantive and procedural values. For example, one asserts that science has reinforced her previously held values by supporting her belief in a divine design of creation (a substantive belief), while another asserts that science has reinforced his belief that life should be a continual quest for truth (a procedural value). Some interpret beliefs and values in a purely moral and theological sense (his ideas of creation were challenged by evolutionary theory) while others interpret the terms more broadly as, for example, belief in certain older and recently revived agricultural practices or belief in either a psychological or genetic and biochemical basis for obesity. A few of our respondents think that, because science can neither deal with nor answer questions of value, it has neither reinforced nor challenged any of their prior beliefs and values. Most, however, are successful in interpreting the findings of science in ways that tend to reinforce and support the beliefs and value structures they were brought up to accept. Even those who have been prompted to rethink prior beliefs in light of science's picture of the world concede only that, while science may "challenge," it does not "threaten" the set of beliefs on which their lives are grounded.

Only two respondents are positive in their judgment of scientists' sensitivity to ethical issues, and of these two, one simply "would hope that most scientists are sensitive" to moral issues, and has "a generally positive" (although not particularly well-informed) feeling on the subject. A majority of the respondents, however, doubt the ethical sensitivity of most scientists. Two general reasons are offered for this judgment. First, scientists are "arrogant," "dogmatic," "so determined to find an end result that they will misrepresent facts to obtain that result," and "so oriented toward collecting the data and conducting the studies" that they have no time for ethical concerns. Second, since scientists are neither better nor worse than other human beings, and since our society is "morally corrupt," scientists are as likely as anyone else to be ethically obtuse or insensitive. Again, the finger is pointed specifically at environmental scientists whose social agenda and "alarmist" attitudes "pervert the appropriate goals of science." Once more, we find the peculiar situation of a population that believes strongly that science has greatly improved life still harboring deep mistrust of the motives and ethical awareness of many scientific practitioners.

Despite their gloomy views of the ethical standards of scientists, our conservative respondents have little knowledge of specific ethical transgressions. But even though the whole group collectively could come up with but a single example of scientific misconduct (the rivalry in AIDS research resulting in improper claiming of credit), there was no hesitation in assigning causes to ethical infractions. "Competitiveness," "professional pressures," "the search for money, fame, and prestige," "indifference and carelessness," and "misrepresenting facts in order to satisfy a political agenda" were all listed as causes of scientific misconduct. The one respondent who has strong positive feelings about the ethical standards and sensitivity of scientists believes that "cheating is a sign of desperation," and that only a small number succumb to the temptation to cheat because of "the pressure to publish."

To discover whether such attitudes toward science are rooted in the conduct of basic or applied research, subjects were asked whether, ideally, the goal of science should be "to learn about the natural world" or "to apply such knowledge to modify nature and use it to achieve human ends." Half the respondents say that "ideally, pure knowledge and applications of this knowledge should be combined; science is a marriage of basic knowledge and applications." But despite their widespread identification of technologies (rather than pure science) as having improved life and "made it better," almost as many believe that the search for pure knowledge should be science's prime goal. They say "science should be purely theoretical; it is not up to scientists to apply knowledge" and "it is up to science to inform, to discover causes; it is not necessarily up to them to propose solutions." The reason for this view seems to be that "solutions [to applied issues] are political, and scientists should probably not be policy makers." It is ironic that a mistrust of scientists' political abilities and motives should account for the idealized view of science as the search for pure knowledge. Only one respondent insists that the prime goal should be application "using knowledge for human benefit."

We went on to relate their ideas about basic and applied research specifically to the issue of improving the quality of the environment. We asked whether we should seek to achieve environmental improvement by introducing gradual, modest, and voluntary changes, such as increased recycling and fuel efficiency, or if we should follow a more radical and draconian path, which would mandate such drastic changes as enforced reduction in the use of air-conditioning, herbicides and pesticides, and automotive transportation. The overwhelming choice was gradualism—for a variety of reasons. A dominant theme was that more radical approaches would confer increased power on political entities, which could ban and prohibit arbitrarily. Science was viewed as functioning in a political and economic context, with "environmental extremists peddling fear and terror to fulfill their political agendas." In such a situation, scientists become pawns of politically motivated environmental extremists.

A second theme was that gradualism is preferable on purely pragmatic grounds because our society will not accept radical solutions, "radical approaches don't work," and "gradualism is less traumatic economically." One respondent viewed radical measures as a manifestation of "liberal" anti-technologism. His faith in technology made him reject the "path of bicycle transportation." He believes that science and technology thrive when there are population and other pressures to innovate, and is sharply critical of the widespread lack of faith in our ability to solve techno-economic problems. "We should use fossil fuels as long as they last, and when the crunch comes we will devise new solutions."

This respondent's technological optimism contrasts with the ideas of the one subject in the conservative group whose ideas are mostly at variance with those of fellow conservatives. This subject maintains that "gradualism in cleaning up the environment doesn't work," suggesting, like Emerson, that "gradualism in theory is perpetuity in practice." Rather than expressing a set of ideas that characterize most of our respondents (economic and social conservatism, strong religious commitment, and skepticism about the motives of scientists), this subject combines political libertarianism with Ross Perot reformism, religious liberalism, fiscal conservatism, and a strongly idealistic view of science and scientists.

In the context of these views of environmental change, we then asked whether leadership in the solution of environmental problems should principally be the responsibility of scientists or of concerned citizens at the grassroots level. While there was widespread agreement that the contributions of both groups are needed, the overwhelming sentiment was that citizens, not scientists, should play leadership roles. A repeated theme was that environmental leadership is fundamentally political in nature, and therefore should not be in the hands of an entrenched scientific elite. "Scientists are no better or worse than anyone else, but policy making is not their bag." Policy making, in other words, should be the prerogative of the people. This suspicion and mistrust of scientists' motives and agendas was emphasized by one respondent who, while recognizing the need for the contributions of scientists, asserted that "we must check out the background of scientists as a guide to their credibility."

To the degree that scientists would probably be agents of governmental bureaucracies, they should be denied leadership roles. Individual and voluntary responsibility for inaugurating action at the local level was stressed. "Not government. The people must do it. Government never does a good job. Too much bureaucracy." Only one respondent in this group opted for leadership from scientists, presumably because of their professional expertise. Most of the rest were unwilling to place their faith in scientific leadership, largely because this sort of leadership would lead to manipulation by extremists and entrenched political interests.

We explored our respondents' perceptions of the scientists' motives and attitudes by asking whether they thought scientists were sympathetic, unsympathetic, or indifferent to such varied environmental organizations as the Sierra Club, the Audubon Society, and Greenpeace. Most believe scientists to be sympathetic, in general, to environmental groups, but the sympathy was viewed as not very strong or compelling. Several thought there was likely to be great variation among scientists in the degree of their sympathy, and one thought that "while scientists are probably not very sympathetic to these groups, they are made to seem sympathetic by the demands of their jobs." Here again we see surfacing the suspicion that scientists are manipulable and likely to subserve the ends and goals of unnamed political groups that exercise control over them.

We moved next to some of the questions raised by both equity and postmodern feminists about the place of women in science. What, we asked, was the effect on choice of research topics of the male domination of science during most of the nineteenth and twentieth centuries? Most believed that there was little or no effect. One said that there was "only a minor impact on choice of topics." This respondent claimed further (and slightly irrelevantly) that "there are no real institutional barriers to women in science." Others commented as follows.

- "In general, the things scientists study are not gender specific."
- "I can't think of any examples illustrating the effect on choice of problems in science having been mainly a male enterprise."

A few did think there has been some effect. "Women's medical issues may have taken second place to AIDS, a predominantly male disease. AIDS research costs as much as [research on] all other diseases combined, practically. Breast cancer takes a backseat to AIDS research." The effect of male domination of science on research topic choice was not, however, a particularly salient issue, even among those who believed that gender did affect choice.

A follow-up question concerned the probable effects of an increased presence of women in the scientific professions. A significant minority of the respondents believed that there would be minimal effects. One person saw no effect except that of a larger number of people fighting over the distribution of limited research funds. The majority who did predict some changes emphasized the effects of traditional and stereotypical "feminine" qualities on the conduct of science. "Since women do not see as men do," women's increased presence will "open new possibilities." They will provide "a more balanced approach" and will "complement present approaches." None of these judgments was illustrated or exemplified by concrete predictions of the character of behavioral changes anticipated. The only specific prediction was that "just as women in journalism bring greater awareness of rape, child care, and sexual battery, more women in science will bring greater awareness of problems special for women; specifically there will be greater advances against diseases which women experience." Breast cancer was the one example cited.

This view of expected change was grounded, in the view of several respondents, in the basic God-created difference between women and men. In contradiction to the feminist view of differences between the genders as socially constructed and enforced, the politically conservative group noted that "women do not see as men do," "women have more of an intuitive approach," and "women bring more sensitivity" to problems.

As the discussion focused more specifically on male and female approaches to doing science, two of the respondents in this group insisted that scientific methods are not amenable to changes induced by the gender of the scientist. "It is the scientific method that determines how people do scientific work. The only effect will be if women's scientific work gets politicized by the feminist movement." This comment echoed the view, expressed in another context, of science and scientists being politicized and manipulated by special interest groups. Another response was that "it would be condescending to think that women's approach to science would differ from men's." The theme is that scientific method is independent of gender.

Yet several of the respondents insisted that, "because God made women different from men," in their scientific work women would be more compassionate and would "think more with their emotions." This would be particularly true in the areas of animal rights and the environment. "Our creator made men and women different, and this difference will certainly have an effect on women's approach to science. Women's way of thinking is . . . more emotional." One respondent did not specify God as the author of the differences, but insisted that, neurophysiologically, "men are more rational, linear, analytical; women are more fluid and intuitive."

Whether these perceived differences are innate or not, they do, according to one respondent, become internalized as a result of a socialization process, and consequently affect work style. This framing then becomes an accepted part of women's role, so that one female respondent was able to say that "women are more used to repetitive work." Then, making a virtue of necessity, it was asserted that "they become more persevering, more used to taking setbacks in stride and going on. Women can hang in there. They bring patience and order and perseverance to their tasks."

Clearly, radical and militant feminism are anathema to this group, which, on balance, is willing to accept what they believe to be innate differences between the sexes, even though there is some disagreement as to whether or not the methods of science permit a range of styles of research grounded in the gender of the scientist. Animal rights and environmental preservation are then viewed as more "feminine" issues, since they are more likely than other areas of scientific work to be appealing to women's more emotional, intuitive, and compassionate natures.

We moved from this topic to the question of big and little science. Has the post–World War II move from little to Big Science benefited society? While there was some acknowledgment of benefits—more money is available for expensive research equipment and some research must be done by teams of scientists who require major resources—the dominant tone was that, insofar as Big Science necessarily involves government, it should, on many grounds, be viewed with suspicion.

- "Government's role is too all-powerful in Big Science."
- "Government sources will accept the ruling paradigm, and this is bad for science. Science thrives in a pluralistic, private environment. Also, we have suffered a loss of high quality undergraduate teaching because of so much government support of research."

Others do not analyze the effects in such detail, but simply maintain that "the entry of government [into research] has not benefited science or society." Government-supported research means politically motivated research.

- "Government tends to manipulate facts. Big Science has not benefited society. You lose originality. A small lab, even today, can come up with an original focus."
- "Government has no business in our lives."

On the other hand, some respondents are willing to accept government support, but not direction. "It's okay for the government to support research as long as there's no interference with the scientific work." Individuals count most in the conduct of research. What government labs can do is continuing (developmental) and scale-up work. There is some acknowledgment of the need for both big and little science, but an undertone of suspicion of government clouds and confuses the picture of the link between Big Science and government.

When asked directly about whether government has the responsibility to fund scientific research, there is near unanimous rejection or, at best, suspicion of this role for government.

- "There is no governmental responsibility to fund scientific research."
- "Government is not to be trusted. Its responsibility is very limited; it should exist only when individuals, private groups, and states can't do it for themselves."
- "Private corporations are better as a source of support than government."
- "Government-funded research, in the form of NASA, for example, has yielded small benefits, relatively."

There was some acknowledgment that both public and private entities have responsibilities in the area of funding. "Balance is needed; science is driven by dreamers as well as practical problems." But the acceptance of government's role seems always to be accompanied by the completely unrealistic view that it is possible for government to supply resources but to abjure any power of guidance or control. "When government support is given, there should be no interference." "Some governmental support is okay as long as there are no strings attached."

On the other hand, there was near-unanimous support in this group for private corporate support of research.

- "Private corporation support of university research prepares students for 'real world' work."
- "Private support is okay. The profit motive is behind private research support, and that's okay."
- "Private corporations are better as a source of support than government."

- "There is much greater appeal to the idea of private than of public support of research."

Some mild reservations, however, were expressed. "There should be no question of manipulation of scientists by donors of funds." Private support is all right "as long as there are no strings attached; no special interests." "Private funding is okay but not as the sole support, since we need dreamers as well as 'nose to the grindstone' research workers." This respondent apparently believes that private support will be for applied projects, but that there is a need for public support of basic projects and "dream stuff."

One respondent opposes both government and corporate support, since the motives of both government and the corporate world are suspect. "With large organizations [either public or private] involved there are problems in entertaining new ideas."

The final area of inquiry involved the relationships between religion and science. Are the two belief systems basically compatible or incompatible? The majority of the political conservatives give strong support to the view that the two are compatible, consistent, and complementary. Since God's moral law governs both the spiritual and the material universes, there can be no incompatibility between good science and good theology. In the words of one respondent, "Good science can correct bad theology; good theology can correct bad science."

Another respondent asserts that "science tries to explain, and the goal of religion is the same. In their explanatory roles, religion and science can complement one another."

A majority of the political conservatives appear to hold orthodox, if not fundamentalist, religious beliefs. Since God is the author of all, there must be a basic and mutual consistency among all His works. "If God created the world, He created laws of matter and energy, and gave us the interest in and capability of discovering them." When investigations in the areas of religion and science are honest and sincere, there is total compatibility.

While these views are held by a majority of the conservatives, they are not unanimous convictions. At least two respondents see some degree of incompatibility. One respondent has a general feeling that the two are probably incompatible because they operate in different spheres. Another extends her political bias against large organizations to religious as well as secular bodies. Churches have denied useful—presumably scientific—knowledge in the name of religion or humanity, and thus may deprive people of the fruits of scientific investigation. In asserting this, this respondent reiterates her mistrust of large organizations, whether governmental, corporate, or religious.

The question of whether religion or science has become more important in the last generation elicited a very mixed response. One respondent sees a falling away from both religious belief and scientific rationality, in favor of a kind of mindless anti-intellectualism. Another, rather than viewing religion and science as allies against anti-intellectualism and ignorance, sees a perpetuation of tension between the two, centered largely on the issue of evolution and creationism. If anything, he believes that evolution has been slightly discredited in the last generation. A stronger statement of this belief was expressed by a respondent who sees the evolution-creationism controversy as a principal source of mutual mistrust. "Evolutionists are more 'liberal' in their ideas. Evolution is just a theory; it is not supported by evidence or facts. Parents must undo what children learn from textbooks of science." According to this view, it is parental rejection of evolution that is responsible for turning the tide of the last generation more to religion than science in recent years. Several see a resurgence of religious belief and spirituality in recent years, though science is still the more dominant force. One somewhat atypical conservative asserted that religion "wants us to go backwards. It is fearful of science. On the question of abortion, religion has regressive attitudes." But the regressiveness has less to do with the moral content of the issue than with the conviction that government should stay out of people's private lives and that, regardless of one's convictions about the morality of abortion, conservative thought demands governmental neutrality on what is ultimately a private issue.

Two respondents reiterated the need for mutual accommodation between science and religion. "Students recognize that science does not have all the answers. There should be a balance between science and religion." The blame for some of the tension rests with the mass media. "There is a difference between what Darwin said and what journalists say Darwin said," implying greater compatibility than the popular press is willing to grant. Another respondent believes that science and religion should "stand side by side," but that neither seems able to accept the other. Mutual fear and insecurity cause this problem. These can be diminished by people with integrity and honesty in both camps, as long as they recognize that both are continually in search of truth.

From this general discussion of the roles of religion and science in modern life, we moved to a series of linked questions about whether teachers should be able to express their religious beliefs in science classes and classes that deal with health and human sexuality in colleges and universities, and in elementary and secondary schools.

A majority of respondents believe that teachers already have or, if they do not, *should have* this right. But several qualified their answers: They should have this right but no such right is absolute; teachers must be sure to identify such expressions as their own opinions and not to integrate them into the course work and present them as received wisdom; students as well as teachers should have this right in a democratic society. The tone of the responses suggested that religious thought should not be viewed or treated differently from other areas of thought. A minority of respondents, however, questioned the advisability of permitting expression of religious opinions in either science or health and human sexuality classes.

While the same general answer was given about religion in elementary and secondary classes, a tone of greater caution was expressed. One respondent felt that, in society generally, "the abortion industry has the freedom to promote its political agenda. There should be opportunities to have all sides of issues presented." Her solution, however, was not to extend opportunities to opposition groups, but rather to abolish all classroom discussion in these sensitive areas. Education about sexuality and family planning is the responsibility of parents; these subjects should not be discussed at all in elementary and secondary schools. One respondent suggested privatization of public education as the solution. It would keep parents in charge; teachers should be the servants of parents.

Once more, while a minority of respondents opposed the introduction of religious opinion into any elementary or secondary classes, the predominant tone was accepting of reasonable expression of religious opinion at every level.

- "Only if it is presented and identified as personal opinion."
- "Okay in elementary and secondary classes if you present all sides; this provokes thought and forms ideas."
- "We must have multiple perspectives at all educational levels."
- "The classroom should be open to all opinions, but there should be no forcing or shaming or indoctrination. All should have the right of free expression. In honesty and respect all should feel free to express their opinions."

A final question concerned the teaching of evolution and of creationism in science classes at all levels. This is a telling issue, since the community of biologists is close to unanimous about evolutionary theory as the fundamental conception upon which all contemporary biology—genetics, microbiology, embryology, developmental and structural biology, biochemistry, and so on—is founded. Despite the overwhelming opinion of life scientists that creationism is a religious rather than a scientific idea, almost all the respondents supported the teaching of both evolution and creationism at all levels.

- "It should be done as long as there is fair and equal treatment of both evolution and creationism."
- "In all fairness, all viewpoints should be presented."
- "Both views should be presented side by side; the truth will ultimately prevail."
- "We need to have all information set out. Then students will make deci-

sions on the basis of what is offered. There should be openness to all sides."

Only two respondents had reservations. One simply said he was opposed to presenting both evolutionary and creation theory in classes at every level, but was unclear as to whether both concepts or merely creationism should be banned. Another, while viewing the Bible as a man-made document subject to interpretation, finally came down on the side of presenting both theories because "it is the individual responsibility of the student to make choices." In this case, individual freedom and responsibility are higher values than the value of keeping biology classes free of what, in her opinion, was non-scientific material.

On the basis of our interviews, we can conclude that political conservatives do not speak with a single voice on all issues, although certain themes and attitudes do play dominant roles in their thinking. Among the most strongly expressed ideas was a mistrust of public institutions, chiefly the federal government and the public schools. While greater confidence was expressed in private schools and private corporations, there was an undertone of suspicion of any and all large institutions and organizations. Individual responsibility was stressed throughout.

There seemed to be scant support for any kind of feminist thought, although modest equity feminism was acceptable to most respondents. The greatest suspicion was aimed at radical environmental science.

By and large, science as an institution and, especially, technology as one of its practical manifestations received reasonably strong support. But science as an institution was more highly esteemed than were individual scientists. The reason seems to be that the principles and methods of science are well established and have been shown to confer ample benefits on society, whereas individual scientists have the potential of operating in league with socially dangerous forces, such as radical environmentalism. Perhaps the greatest fear was the corruption or manipulation of scientists by liberal or otherwise unsavory political forces. This interesting synthesis combined respect and regard for science as an institution with considerable suspicion of its practitioners.

Reflections from the Political Left

"I am very pessimistic about the future. In fact lately I have been thinking I'm glad I'm forty-six years old because maybe I'll live out my life before the entire thing goes bad. I figure it's for sure, it's already too late. There's going to be a gigantic disaster and I don't see any way around it."

My parents are middle of the road. They are mostly Democrat, but my father once voted for Eisenhower. I'm from a Catholic background, which you can attribute to my parents. When my parents became aware of my politics, I wouldn't say they were flabbergasted or thought I was an idiot. But it was a major change. It wasn't something my parents believed.

I don't believe that there are any large organized groups in the United States that share my politics. There's no left-wing political party. Some of the European parties are more socialist oriented and I could identify with them. Aside from politics, there is a group of physicists who send me their literature. I did get involved with them on the nuclear freeze movement. I really was very active. When I came to work [at the university], it was me and two other guys who were handing out literature about nuclear freeze in the physics department. But I'm not a member of the Union of Concerned Scientists. I got their literature for a while, but I don't anymore.

My politics affects some of my thinking as a scientist. I am more likely to look for the material interests behind what we do, like the interests of the groups that fund and dominate physics, or those groups that have the money and power to get their way. But when you come to actual scientific problems, and you're looking for the right answers, I don't think my politics has any influence. Right now my politics leads me to be concerned about the way people treat post-docs and graduate students. A big issue is that physics is really up the creek because there are no jobs, at least not in academic physics. What's our responsibility to the grad students we accept and train? Do we just take them and use them and say "tough luck" if they can't get a job? It's on issues like this that my politics intervenes, kind of like when you support minimum-wage legislation, because this is a labor issue. Is it really ethical to bring in all those suckers, and they TA for a lousy wage for two years, they get a Ph.D., and then what actually happens to them? In some ways it's in our selfish interest to get these guys, use them as TAs, but is it really in their interest to do it? It's hard for me to be totally idealistic because I don't want to have to start teaching recitation sections either. I'm just saying it's tough to know what to do.

The kind of society I would like to live in would be organized along socialist lines, where people can develop their abilities as far as they can, and the products of labor are shared equitably among people. No one is in want. And the other element for me is that things have to be democratic, so that people have some say-so about what happens. I don't know what role science can play in the development of that kind of society. Maybe science can contribute to greater productivity, so that once you produce enough stuff it is easier to share it and be fair. But other than that, I don't think science has much to do with it, at least not hard science. Social science, if they could ever figure anything out, might have more significance.

Another way that politics gets into science has to do with the power of experts versus democratic decisions about scientific questions. It's hard to say what's best because there are certain questions for which you really have to know what you're doing to say what is right. Take the question of climate change. One group of experts says one thing and another group disagrees. This gets you into the politics of the professions, who gets promoted, and who gets funded. Maybe if you left the atmospheric scientists alone for twenty years to battle it out, they would finally come up with the right answer just among themselves. Does science produce the correct answer internal to itself? The problem is that finding answers is not that clear-cut. In fact, I strongly disagree with a colleague who is in favor of nuclear power. There are two reasons for my disagreement with him. The first is that scientists can be naïve. If six Nobel Prize winners were running the plant, that would be fine with me. But in real life it's some alderman in Chicago and his mafia buddies who are pouring the concrete, and it's going to be bought from some crummy guy in concrete. In other words, I think our society's too corrupt to keep up with the standards that nuclear power would need. That's not anything a physicist can judge, right? That's my opinion about our society. On a technical level it should work—and if I trusted the guys running it, but I don't trust them. The second reason is more sympathetic to my colleague, who is an experimentalist. Good experimentalists have to have optimistic attitudes when they are going to do difficult experiments. They have to believe that they can overcome problems that arise. That's a good attitude to have if you're an experimentalist, but that very quality can make them overly rosy about nuclear power.

Some people have a more optimistic attitude about American society, but I'm very pessimistic. Between all the trees getting chopped down and the pollution—and you can't find a street in the United States now that doesn't have pesticides in it. That's very unstable. So for me it's obvious.

The whole thing is going to crap out. There's going to be big epidemics of diseases and deaths and starvation. What we need is a major restructuring of our society, but I don't think it will happen. We are too disorganized and you'll never convince people to do it. But I think it's already too late.

Some people think religion has a positive role to play in confronting some of our problems. I don't know because religion is such a double-edged sword for me. You can be happy one day when the pope uses his power for some progressive cause and the next day you can be dismayed when he uses that same power for some ridiculous cause. I donate money to the American Friends Service Committee, who are Quakers in some sense. They're the least Christian religious group you can imagine, and they are a group where religion seems positive. For me, I don't know what to think about religion.

It is hard to say what the public's view of science is. The general man or woman in the street, what does he or she think? On the one hand, you seem to think that when people read in the paper what scientists say, it seems to carry weight. On the other hand, despite what their doctors tell them, they spend millions of dollars on herbal medicines. When it really should count, when it comes to their health, the public doesn't follow official science, they do what they want. It's kind of like the Middle Ages, when people would go to church and then go outside and do some superstitious thing to cover their bases. I'm just saying, it's one thing for people to talk about science and another to literally act like they believe it. I don't know if this reflects skepticism of science. I get the feeling that with young people, they don't care about science either way.

I know that there are big disputes today between humanists and scientists. Some of the physics guys don't appreciate what the humanists are trying to do when they write about science. When you're doing science you have the feeling that there's some objective thing out there and that in some way you are learning about the world which is independent of us. What scientists resent is that they feel the humanists don't recognize this touching reality, which is the happiest moment—when you have something non-trivial to say about the way the real world works. I think that both sides are dodging the most interesting issue. The extreme positions are both trivial. If there really isn't an objective world and it's all just socially created, that's kind of trivial. And if there is an objective world, and there is no political and social side to science, that's also trivial. The deep question is, how is it that both things are true? It's socially created, but it's grasping an element of reality, which I think is the real case.

Chapter 5

Political Left and Science Corrupted

Michael Dennis

The political left looks at science through a lens that is highly critical of capitalism as an economic system and very dubious about the actions of corporations within that system. Capitalism, with its emphasis on free markets, consumerism, and putting profits before people, is seen as having the capacity to corrupt the practice of science. Corporations are the instrument of that corruption because they seek out the knowledge produced by science in order to transform it into profitable products. When science gets caught in the web of profit-seeking corporations, the result is a corrupted science.

Our interviews with members of progressive, left-leaning organizations reveal divergent patterns of thought and much critical commentary about science. Their views also provide the conclusion that they largely accept and welcome the contributions of science. In fact, the responses of the political left are consistent with the hypothesis that members of special interest groups perceive science-related problems only to the extent that such problems intersect with their respective groups' interests. Science-related issues that trouble feminists, environmental activists, and religious fundamentalists do not seem to create much anxiety for this group of critics. Instead, when prompted to react to specific deficiencies in modern science, defenders of the political left do so moderately, and predictably place culpability for science's ills at corporate America's doorstep.

GENERAL CONFIDENCE IN SCIENCE

The political left sees science as having noble goals and great potential for contributing quality-of-life improvements. Scientific misconduct and negative side effects of science-based technologies are explained away as by-products of science's ties to corporations. At least as an entity unto itself, science is not an institution under siege from this group of political leftists with experiences in a variety of liberal, progressive, and socialist political organizations. Indeed, these respondents show little interest in attacking science itself.

This is not to say that our respondents fully trust science or condone the entire agendas of its practitioners and researchers. In fact, they are reluctant to place too much faith in the judgment and leadership of scientists on important issues. However, when there are such objections concerning the inner workings and/or outcomes of American science, our panel is likely to implicate and indict corporate funding as the negative influence. Thus, the mercenary considerations to which science answers bear the brunt of criticisms offered by the leftist sample.

The mostly favorable reactions to science described above are actually contrary to the general experiences these subjects had in their earlier direct contacts with science course work. While one found high school and college engineering courses "positive and interesting," he also soon turned to the social sciences and became a psychology major. Others found that despite "wanting to like them," science courses were "boring," "uninteresting," "unremarkable," and "both difficult and intimidating." The one person in the sample with an extensive background in science had more positive associations with science course work as he progressed through the levels of degrees pursued. Current interest in science among the other non-scientists ranged from "ambivalent" and "minimal" to "enjoying reading just the conclusions."

No respondent felt that life was worse as a result of scientific advances. Most acknowledged science as a mixed bag of positive and negative results, and at least one stated unequivocally that science had made life better.

- "The results are both productive and exploitative."
- "It's a mixed bag. Medical research is a boon, while applications in agriculture have created pesticide pollution in addition to upping production. There's an element of the Frankenstein myth to it."
- "Life-expectancy increases, quality of life, the onset of computer advancements, and expansion of leisure time and comforts are definite good points."
- "Thanks to science and its promotion, I finally was able to quit smoking."

Positive statements about science were often modified with a caveat about the institutional context in which science is conducted. It is this context, rather than science itself, that is responsible for many of the negative effects.

- "The problem with science and technology is that they are owned by private corporations. The harmful effects are caused by capitalism. If science and technology were owned by the working class they would change dramatically."

Those who were able to provide cases where science either supported or weakened their belief systems decided that their value systems were strengthened by such encounters, if affected at all. One educator who also serves in a political office in the community was sure that "science reinforces beliefs" but was hard pressed to provide an example. Eventually, she used the practice of washing one's hands before eating as both a valued practice and a belief upheld by science's findings. Most took this line of questioning in more spiritual directions.

- "I had my own philosophical disputes with religion and didn't need science to challenge them, although it could have."
- "If I had creationist beliefs, they'd be threatened by science."
- "I was conflicted. Science eventually contributed to my loss of religion."

The last respondent above said later in the interview that he believes religion does more harm than good. Indeed, at least in their own estimations, none seem to be the worse for wear given their de-emphasizing, or even abandonment of, religion, regardless of science's role in their anti-conversions.

When asked about their confidence in the findings of science, they generally provide a qualified expression of confidence. The qualifications reflect an understanding that the process of developing knowledge is fraught with uncertainty.

- "I will tell you that I am a skeptic. That means I am uncomfortable with what I hear from scientific experts and specialists. I'm not sure that what we get is quote-unquote the truth, or some variation or shading or interpretation of what we might call the truth. I don't believe everything I hear, but that doesn't bother me because science is continuously an investigating, ongoing process."

This is similar to their reactions to the presence of scientific controversies, which does not shake their faith in the institution's credibility, but, rather, is expected as part and parcel of the nature of science's movement toward progress.

- "Scientists do the best they can at the moment. They resolve it, hopefully, with fact gathering and interpretation."

- "I see the whole process of science as including mistakes. I respond positively to science's controversies. It is the nature of science."
- "I'd have to say 'Yes' and 'No' as to having confidence in science. It grows with replication. I don't trust individual reports as much as a body of knowledge. I'll wait for the body of evidence before accepting it."
- "I always lean toward the preponderance of evidence, especially in the absence of personal interest. The majority of science does not have immediate social or economic implications. It's all right to trust those results."
- "While I do have a general confidence in science, I distrust social science and the role of corporate America. Most of the disagreements that emerge are political in nature and interest-laden."

The above reference to distrust of "the role of corporate America" marks our initial observation of the political left's critical skepticism toward commercial interest in science. Such concerns are more evident in response to queries about scientists' ethics and potentials for engaging in acts of misconduct. Only one respondent lauded the ethics of scientists, labeling them "ethical by the nature of what they do."

Another felt they should receive only a grade of C on their ethical report cards. Others thought that scientists were "not necessarily ethical." This may stem from the belief that "scientists can be bought." Most of our panel offered outright indictments of scientists and their findings' dependence on "dollar sign science."

- "Some scientists are bought. Those hired by Monsanto, the chemical company, and the tobacco and oil companies find that growth hormones and smoking are harmless and that there is no such thing as global warming."
- "Scientists may delude themselves and do illegitimate science for corporate interests."

In some cases, actual misconduct, as defined by the standards of science, occurs in laboratories. This can range from reporting of only hypothesis-consistent results to actual and purposeful fabrication of data. Our panel is mostly aware of the existence of such malpractice and is willing to ascribe two types of ignoble reasons for it. Not surprisingly, corporate influence is often presumed to be a causal factor.

- "It's capitalism that biases result toward favorable outcomes."
- "Often it's due to big money interests."
- "The Wall Street pigs exert control over science."

- "Some cases have to do with money, obtaining research funding. Some have to do with ego and the driving passion for money, prestige, and fame."

While only one respondent was unaware of and uninformed about scientific misconduct, all others were knowledgeable and even distinguished different levels of it. Several blamed ambition, and one mentioned possible racial bias.

- "I'm interested in malpractice and follow it somewhat in *Science* magazine. They're my favorite articles. There are different levels from willful bad things to just lack of objectivity. They come about because of career stresses and personal aspects."
- "I've heard of data fabrication and imagine it's caused by ego involvement, pressure, and prestige requirements."
- "There's more misconduct in social science. Ambition and the pressures of the academic environment are to blame, although I'm sure I could invent political reasons if I had to."
- "Scientists know they can make their reputations on falsified data."
- "I can recall a case in California where an older patient was helped to die because they wanted to use her body parts. Many black people will not indicate on their license that their body parts can be used if they are seriously injured in an accident. They are afraid that some doctors might be too eager to let them die."

When our respondents discussed the goals of science, they were asked to consider the question of whether science should have basic, knowledge-gaining purposes or be driven by the quest to utilize scientific information in the name of progress. Two respondents ducked the question, one opted for applied science, one liked the goal of pure science, two chose a combination of the alternatives, and one provided a third goal for science.

- "I don't like this basic-versus-applied stuff. Science should help save the planet!"
- "The goal should be to better understand and live more harmoniously with nature."
- "I see both ends as goals of science. I resist that dichotomy."
- "Science should be applied so as to improve the human condition."
- "We need to learn more about nature and worry about modifying the environment less."
- "Applied science should be the goal, but corporate funding of science doesn't allow the meeting of pure goals or applications for all of society."

- "There's a third rationale for science—to learn in order to control nature. To control is different from just applying knowledge for human ends. I don't look at science and scientific development as strictly beneficent. There is a relationship between science and power."

Even the casual reader should note the impingement of environmental concerns into responses about the goals of science. Preserving and improving our relationship with nature appears to be what this sample has in mind as a primary responsibility for scientists. It does not seem, however, to be the case that this group laments the degree to which science is performing that responsibility. The following section describes their opinions on scientists' dedication to environmental concerns and their role in leading environmental movements, as well as their own preferences for different social routes to environmental responsibility.

NATURE, SCIENCE, AND CHANGE

On the whole, respondents do not see scientists as either particularly sympathetic or antagonistic to environmental organizations. Two respondents had absolutely no opinion as to whether scientists are sympathetic to Greenpeace, the Audubon Society, the Sierra Club, and other groups. Another stated that some scientists are sympathetic to environmental organizations, while a fourth guessed that it would vary with scientific specialties. The lack of an unqualified consensus is clear.

- "Scientists are unsympathetic to environmental organizations."
- "In my opinion, it varies. For instance, biologists are more liberal than physicists, and it changes with the eras they are from. But the biologists are likely to be more sympathetic."
- "Scientists at [this large Midwestern university] who will work for the military are very unsympathetic to the environmental organizations."
- "Depends on the scientist. I don't want to categorize them as all the same. Many are indifferent or antagonistic."

Respondents did not show a particularly intense disposition toward taking radical steps to protect the natural environment. If societal change is indeed to be implemented to benefit to the environment, they were asked, should the nature of that change be gradual, such as improvements in recycling and fuel efficiency, or more drastic, as with radical lifestyle changes to reduce consumption of energy?

Whereas the least inhibited of the respondents on this issue was "absolutely for the radical approach to change," the rest saw merit in both avenues of change.

- "Radical and gradual change are not necessarily exclusive."
- "While I see the value of both, the gradual approach may not have effects other than easing our collective consciousness, while the radical, if not carefully selected, can alienate sections of society and thwart progress."
- "Although gradual improvements are certainly needed, we must move as fast as feasible. I'm against having a recycling police, but we should move faster than gradually."
- "I like the hard and the easy solutions. We could live with less, or no air-conditioning. To improve though, just padlock the Pentagon. A Communist Party plank is to take the profit owners out of energy. We can wean ourselves off oil and democratize its control. Instead of just getting rid of cars, we could restructure civilization. It's too bad [Ronald] Reagan ended research on alternative fuels."
- "Often, both approaches are in operation. Maybe the more drastic approach comes when there's a perception of crisis."

For a supposedly political-left group, their endorsement of radical change to instill environmental protection was less than overwhelming. This is, perhaps, an indication of their lack of interest in environmental issues. Finally, assuming that someone must lead the environmental charge, the sample was asked to point to the proper sources of such leadership, if given the choice between scientists and the involvement of increasingly concerned citizens. Leadership by scientists was not a popular choice, and no respondent was willing to bestow unqualified leadership on them.

- "The leadership should come mostly from citizens. Scientists should get involved in grassroots movements if they want to help."
- "It's a political reality that society won't give scientists the power to decide. This is probably good. We do need scientists, though, to ensure informed decisions."
- "Leadership should be a balance between science and the body politic."
- "Scientists don't have all the answers. Scientists as experts cannot lead anybody. That is a form of intellectual and cultural domination. I would be in the forefront of those challenging the rise of scientists as experts, and policy or political leaders. I think there is always an interaction between scientists and citizens and policy making. Scientists can be facilitators who aid people to understand how to develop their own voice, so that they can speak in their own interest."
- "I don't think experts should be running people's lives. Ordinary peo-

ple should have the upper hand in matters related to the environment. But knowledge is very important and people have to avail themselves of experts. You can't have a democratic vote on what should be done. You need both the experts and ordinary people."

Obviously, our panel wishes that scientists would support environmental movements and provide knowledge by which they and others can join in effective decision making. However, scientists are also viewed as not particularly enthusiastic about supporting the environmental movement. And if scientists are to be granted leadership on the environmental issues about which the respondents do not seem particularly anxious, our respondents are still motivated to fight against the intrusion of big business in that process.

- "I trust scientists to provide leadership as long as they're not bought by corporate interests."

The next subject required our leftist respondents to discuss the long-established marginalization of women in science, and the anticipated effects of women's recent progress toward increased involvement in the scientific professions. Despite their generally liberal stances the interviewees displayed less prior acknowledgment of, or forethought about, feminist issues and science than might be expected.

WOMEN AND SCIENCE: PAST, PRESENT, AND FUTURE

Interviewers began this line of questioning by stating the assumption that science has traditionally been male-dominated and inquiring as to the implications of such patriarchal tendencies. One respondent took an environmental perspective in providing insight.

- "The lack of women in science has contributed to science's drive to dominate nature and affected what we study."

Moreover, the latter part of this statement reflects the position taken by many respondents, namely that the predominant effect of male-dominated science has been the selection of topics researched.

- "The male dominance has affected, through exclusion, the topics chosen to work on."
- "Most of the medical research has been performed on men and con-

cerns men's health problems. They do cancer and heart research on men because, they say, women's bodies add complicating factors."
- "Sure, it can make a difference. Probably, there are different perspectives provided as a result."
- "Not only the subjects they work on, but their approach to these subjects. For example, in studies of contraception the focus has been on the female body. Why is there no Norplant for men? Another issue is cesarean births. If there were more women doctors, I wonder if there would have been a different approach."

The next logical queries were directed at what the recent and current trends of inclusion of women in science will mean to science and how these changes may come to be. Subjects were asked what the effects of more women will be in the near future, and whether women approach scientific research differently than do men. These mostly male thinkers seem to welcome women into the fold of established science, but are not very creative in envisioning what the consequences will be. At most, they continue to see the topics studied as the central issues, and the value systems injected into the subjective issues of science as potentially altered, with the lessening of the patriarchal stranglehold on science.

- "I imagine women's conditions will be studied more. There will be different values displayed in research agendas."
- "This will lead to broader debates."
- "The obvious answer is that there is an increase in human resources. I think there will be other effects but I'm not sure what they will be."
- "The influx of women into science hopefully will cause research that includes both sexes equally. It should add another perspective on science. Their approach will be different definitely in what they choose to research, and possibly with the values they bring to research."
- "Women will do science differently. [They] will bring different approaches to problems."
- "It seems to me there may be some differences in approach. I guess maybe even to the extent that humane treatment of experimental subjects, in both human and animal subject cases, may be enhanced. But I don't think there has been such a tendency and I don't know to what extent it comes from scientific ideology as such or whether it's a kind of overlay of a patriarchal and dominate-the-earth kind of mentality."
- "I think there are different standpoints between men and women, but I don't want to say that there is some particular natural thing that women will do that is fundamentally different. We can't say that women are natural nurturers when all those women are killing their kids."

As a whole, the political left is much more responsive to and opinionated about the mixture of our nation's political mechanisms and the institution of science than about women's expanding roles within the latter. One exception to the left's general disinterest in fully exploring the ramifications of a less patriarchal science was this young male's speculations, which tie together many of the interview topics.

- "The inequality has contributed a great deal to the drive to dominate nature, rather than to adapt to it. It's also affected what we study. Our civilization is backwards when it comes to sociology, anthropology, philosophy, psychology, and knowledge of the self. We're always very outward looking and that tends to correspond with the attitude that our society describes as masculine. I mean we know so much about particle physics and astronomy. We know so little about how to get the Arabs and Israelis to live next to each other. Yeah, I think more women in science would make a difference."

Perhaps one reason the political left does not see the question of women in science as a hot-button issue is linked to its central concern with economic and political inequalities. Women doctors and women scientists are part of a privileged class in American society, and more often than not, they are tied to powerful organizations that protect their interests. It is hard to imagine our political left respondents expressing much sympathy for doctors who are complaining about how health maintenance organizations (HMOs) are limiting their ability to practice medicine (and, incidentally, limiting their fees). They would be amused by the elite American Medical Association's recent vote to form a union for doctors, because the left would recall the AMA's traditional opposition to any kind of national health care system.

The next set of questions focused on our respondents' reactions to the intrusions of government and business into science's workings. Overall, the responses were decidedly more emphatic than for our previous topics.

POLITICS AND SCIENCE: PREFERRING THE CAPITOL'S CAPITAL

We begin with a contrast of today's Big Science with an earlier time when science was small scale, conducted by individuals or small teams in small laboratories. All of our respondents agreed that science is funded differently now than it was fifty years ago. For instance, government and corporate funding has largely replaced the individual investigator working in his privately sponsored laboratory. Predictably, the left is not enthusiastic about the roles government and corporate funding of Big Science play. None will admit the existence of outright benefits directly traceable to government funding of science, although most recognize the responsibility of the federal government to provide that funding.

- "There probably is more funding now with the shift to government-sponsored science. We need more than just the very affordable research, so the government does have a responsibility to fund it."
- "Government does have a responsibility, although I can't give an answer to whether we benefit from government-funded projects."
- "It's mixed. There are positive and negative aspects. Certainly, there are plenty of technological benefits. Yet there are negative changes related to the incorporation of science within capitalist government and, specifically, the military establishment. The federal government should further and oversee research, if not just outright fund it. The worst examples, such as Hitler's Nazi science, should not chill us from the government-science connection."
- "There have been some benefits from Big Science and some problems. A lot of things that scientists do are in the interest of government, and that may not benefit people."
- "Government science is more beneficial. It means more resources, more combinations of great minds, such as at MIT. However, all military influence leads to useless research. Government is responsible for funding scientific works."
- "Government has as much funding responsibility as any other corporate institution."

Much in line with earlier responses, it is corporate funding that is viewed as responsible for the detrimental aspects of science. The practice of corporations funding university research draws varied and scathing criticism.

- "Private funding skews and distorts functions of universities. I prefer government support of university science over corporate. Universities essentially become agents of corporations. The nature of modern universities is to become extensions of corporations."
- "Results [of corporate-funded science] should always be suspect. . . . I would be very suspicious of the results, if not the motivation, of the scientists, such as the woman who did research on cheeseburgers. Cheeseburgers were supposed to have some ingredient that helps to fight cancer. But the research was funded by someone with a vested interest in our eating cheeseburgers. I would have to see this replicated many times!"
- "Corporations feed off pure science, benefit from it. . . . I don't see cor-

porate-sponsored research addressing the human endeavor, the goals for pure or beneficially applied science."

- "There's a sense in which one of the elements of science's ethos is to pursue knowledge for its own sake, to learn more about the universe and the world and things in it. . . . There still are probably a lot of things that are worth looking into—and you'd probably find a lot of them on the philosophy department's shelves—that people aren't looking into because they're busy doing these other things that have some commercial and military applications."
- "It's okay if it's controlled properly, and that's a problem. It's difficult to do. The idea is, they just provide the funding, we control the science. The problem is that a researcher gets supported by a company and he or she can do whatever he or she wants scientifically, but whether or not his or her funding is going to be continued hangs in the balance."
- "It's a very bad influence. It's a corrupting influence. It skews the results. If a scientist is working for Sweet 'N Low, he's gonna tell you that saccharin is harmless. I don't think corporations have the right to exist. Corporations should be abolished entirely."

Two left respondents fail to make a sharp distinction between government and corporate funding.

- "Corporate funding can compromise the researcher, but there are two reasons not to exclude corporate funding: survival, as universities are hurting for funding, and that companies do actually inspire real-world concerns and research."
- "I'm not going to make an enormous distinction between government financing and corporate financing. There is a tendency for government to reflect the public interest—at least they say that. On the other hand, the private sector's agenda is profit making, and there is the real possibility that scientific research can be shaped and controlled. What they do is more direct, while government has the veneer of working in the public interest."

While there appears to be agreement that the magnitude of science is such that some sort of funding agency is necessary, and that the benefits are sufficient to justify some large expenditures, most seem to feel that government-sponsored research is the way to go, or is at least preferable to the evils the corporate world brings to research. Apparently, the state and science are considered acceptable bedfellows. However, a segment of the left is equally suspicious of both state power and corporate power.

RELIGION AND SCIENCE: MORE COMPATIBLE THAN EXPECTED

The final topic in our interviews is religion and science, and it explores the possibility that much of the perception that science is under siege may be due to the conflict that arises between religious and scientific explanations of the origin of our species. From the left sector, it is expected that science's end of the continuum will draw more sympathy, as it is usually conservatives who tend to anchor their belief systems to (often literal) religious perspectives on the world. It also seems logical that the political left is more likely to expand religious beliefs to accommodate science's contradictory findings. Therefore, they may perceive less incompatibility between the two. It is also expected that left thinkers will see science as having "gained ground" in its sometimes adversarial relationship with religion proper. The assumption about compatibility is only partially upheld, as our respondents answered on each side of the compatibility question.

- "Conservative Christianity and scientific beliefs are incompatible. That fascist Pat Robertson and the Christian Coalition are intellectual know-nothings who pick on targets like academics, '60s radicals, multiculturalists, womens' studies programs, and science, with its concepts like evolution. It's these know-nothings who embrace garbage like *The Bell Curve*'s indictments of blacks."
- "Science is conflicted with religious beliefs, which by the way, do more harm than good. While some forms of Eastern religion and Spinoza's Judaism may be compatible with science, the 'walking corpse' dogma of Christianity certainly is not."
- "While there's nothing necessarily incompatible about having a religious belief and science, [some] given religious beliefs do conflict."
- "At least for me, they're basically compatible."
- "Religion is completely compatible with science. You might say they're complementary. They answer different questions. Science describes and explains the physical, while religion answers spiritual questions."
- "They clearly are compatible, and scientists will tell you that."

While generally expressing mixed opinions on whether science and religion are compatible, the panel is also divided on how the relationship between science and religion has changed over the last generation or so.

- "Science and religion are co-existing better recently. People are dropping some of the religious beliefs to accommodate science."
- "If there's a change in the relationship, it's that they're less at odds."
- "Religion used to be more important than it is now. Some, other than me, might say science has become a religion."

- "In many ways, since the Enlightenment, religion has become less of a public factor. In the last few decades we may be seeing a return to religion, but in my view, it is a politicization of religion. Having said that, science has advanced in its competition—if you want to call it that—with religion."
- "It seems to me that the population at large today has a more unscientific attitude than in earlier days. There seems to be a reversion to superstition, and not valuing what science is and can do. This bothers me because science can be dangerous to an elite that is dominating all areas of society. And if you weaken science you strengthen that elite."

It seems that religion's hold on our value system, according to this sample, is being usurped by science and its competing explanations of the natural world. But how does this view deal with the final questions posed about religion's efforts to infiltrate the science classroom. Subjects were asked, for both high school and college science courses, whether teachers' religious opinions about delicate topics such as sexuality and family planning should be aired. Also, we were interested what role Darwinian evolution and biblical creationism should be allowed to play in the classrooms. No one had a straight, assertive response about professors' and teachers' injection of personal beliefs into lectures.

- "Professors should have the freedom to express religious opinion if clarified as such. As long as identified as religious opinion and not the Truth, it's okay on the college campus and in public schools."
- "Professors' freedoms are not a good idea, but I don't believe in censorship. Professors shouldn't abuse their power to influence. I come down on the side of professional integrity."
- "I'm indecisive on professors' freedoms. On balance, there should be no restrictions. I teach my students that there is no such thing as objectivity anyway."
- "Professors can discuss those issues freely; public-school teachers shouldn't. Either way, using the classroom as a soapbox isn't right. The public school delivers a captive audience. Just the same, children do need birth control and safe-sex instruction."

The level of contradiction in several of the previous responses attests to the equivocation these interviewees feel about the practice of expressing religious opinion in the classroom. Creationism, at least, was roundly found unacceptable, at least in public-school classrooms.

- "Creationism is okay in college, but not in public school, because there is no empirical basis to it."

- "Darwinism is a science, while creationism is a religious viewpoint. It doesn't belong in science classes on either level."
- "Professors should never make students endorse an ism."
- "People should be free to express their opinions, but with younger kids it becomes more of a problem. They are not equipped to assess the opinions they might get. You can't have people using their personal beliefs to reverse a curriculum that has been adopted. This is a very delicate issue."
- "No! If it is not science they shouldn't put it in the science curriculum. I know they sometimes try to make religion look like science in order to get it in."

While the political left is for the expression of personal beliefs, at least in the college classroom, it is also concerned that creationism not be framed within a scientific context. Although the responses to our queries regarding religion, science, and education tended toward our expectations, they drew nothing approaching the invective reserved for the political issues raised above. The left does not object to religion in the university science classroom with any of the vehemence it displays against having corporations in the university laboratory.

CONCLUSION

It seems that our sample of politically active leftists refuses to embrace any institution entirely. Science is found laudable and its accomplishments are recognized, but its vulnerability to the influence of corporate funding is particularly loathed. The panel accordingly believes that not all products and results of science are worthwhile, but they have faith in its epistemologies and abilities to produce well-verified "bodies of evidence."

This group is not particularly motivated, at least not without prodding, to address the feminist or environmentalist agendas as they relate to science, nor is it particularly incensed by the intrusion of science and religion into each other's previous dominions. This does not reflect, however, an unwillingness to acknowledge or even support any of the positions we might label as progressive stances relative to the feminist, environmental, or evolutionary perspectives on science. The respondents just do not seem especially committed to any of these positions. Neither do they appear to be placing science under siege, as a whole, or in the name of any of these particular issues. Rather, these leftists object to the presence of profit-making corporations in the role of sponsors of research. As we would expect from members of this special interest group, they are concerned about science being put in the service of corporate interests rather than science for all the people.

Reflections of a Fundamentalist

"My father often said, 'Son, you may know a lot, and everything you know may be right. But you don't know everything, and you don't know *what* you don't know, and you don't know *that* you don't know what you don't know.' "

You know, I wasn't brought up in the more conservative and more fundamentalist church I serve now. I was brought up in a liturgical church, and my father is probably more liberal right now than I am. But I was always drawn to a more Bible-oriented approach to things. When I was a teenager I became more involved in church life, and at age fifteen I made a commitment to this denomination. What was especially compelling to me was that it offered a perspective on life that was more cohesive and more Bible-oriented, and helped me see how life could be understood and interpreted on the basis of the Bible.

My dad's whole opinion was that people will do what they want to do and try to find their best way through. As my dad dealt with tragedy and frustration, he just learned how to accept moral ambiguity. I wanted more certainty than that in life, so I was attracted to a more Bible-oriented, evangelical approach to things, an approach that gave me that certainty. I was pretty hard-nosed in my opinions in some areas. But I've had a challenging event happen to me in the past year—my marriage has come apart and we're in the process of divorce. You come very unglued by this experience.

As a result of this experience, some of my views have become a little more squishy. I'm not quite as sure as I was about how everything works. The interesting thing is that I'm probably leaning toward my dad's perspective on a few things. Now, I wouldn't want it understood that I'm truly departing from the views I held earlier—that I'm no longer conservative in my overall view of things—but with what I'm facing now in relationships, things aren't quite as solid in my universe as they were earlier. It's been a challenge to reconcile quite a few things.

I've always been interested in finding out how things work and what the world would be like if things worked differently. I think that's why I liked my biology and chemistry courses in high school. They taught me something about why things work as they do. That's useful knowledge for a pastor: to be able to explain how things in the universe work. I remember one science teacher I had in high school who asked us to figure out what the world would be like if ice didn't float. Well, to explore how virtually everything on Earth would be radically different was just fascinating.

The teachings of science and the teachings of the Bible often appear to be incompatible. The scientific and the scriptural accounts of the age of the universe are simply contradictory. Another example: Methuselah, the oldest man mentioned in the Bible, is supposed to have lived 969 years. We don't and can't understand that kind of longevity today. And, as they stand, the scientific and scriptural accounts of the creation seem to be pretty irreconcilable. Now, what do I do when what I learn from science and what I learn from the Bible are inconsistent with each other? I obviously have a very high opinion of the Bible as the word of God—-but I do of science as well—and I have to deal with these apparent contradictions between the two. Well, I have concluded that there are three possible causes for what appear to me at this time to be contradictions: (1) I misunderstand the substance or the implications of certain scientific discoveries; (2) I misunderstand Scripture; or (3) science's understanding is still incomplete and more knowledge will eliminate the apparent contradiction.

This third possibility seems to be built into the very nature of science. That's why I'm not particularly disturbed when scientific specialists disagree with each other. It simply means that what is scientific "truth" can change over time when more information and data are available. That's why I don't have to be overly intimidated when science appears to challenge some of my beliefs. Science is often wrong in the short run—and disagreements can be resolved in the long run. Ultimately, I think science and religion have to be compatible—and it's the job of the pastor to elucidate and reconcile any temporary tension that exists between the two.

But unfortunately, there has been greater polarization in recent years between people with very fundamentalist ideas and those with a pretty strictly scientific approach. Unfortunately, there's been an almost cynical rejection of the public schools by some people on this account. One man I know never calls them "the public schools." He calls them "the government schools." This doesn't help.

Now, are there some kinds of science that just should not be done because they violate ethical or religious mandates? Tough question. One very difficult area is experimentation with fetal tissue. Maybe that kind of research could help us solve some serious practical health problems or some theoretical problems about the origin of life. And yet the use of fetal tissue is profoundly offensive to some people, especially the methods of obtaining that tissue. What is most morally offensive to me is destroying life, whether it's the unborn or those late in life.

Of course, I support science. Science makes life more convenient and more comfortable. We sit in air-conditioned rooms and have antibiotics when we're sick and watch television for amusement. But should science have a blank check from society? Well, I believe that science should be done for practical reasons: to improve people's health, to make them more comfortable, and to use to our advantage the world we were given. I've thought a lot about the question of human dominion over nature as we learn of it in the Book of Genesis. I believe we've been blessed with the world about us and that we have a responsibility as humans to modify it as we see best and then reap the benefits of what we've done. Without application to human needs, science is kind of abstract. Lacks utility. At the same time, I'm aware that some people and some corporations, in pursuit of their goals, have abused the environment and have not protected the health and welfare of their employees. Somehow it's the duty of society as a whole to tell them they can't do that. But in reality, the free market does the job best by making it in the economic self-interest of corporations to protect the environment, and society has to make this happen. It's not always easy to do this, but I believe in the long run the marketplace will work best to make individuals and industry act in society's best interest.

I'm basically optimistic about the future. We all have our trials to cope with, but my religious faith and my belief in the positive results of scientific research give me grounds for optimism.

Chapter 6

Creationism and the Fundamentalist Critique

Our sampling of a group of religious fundamentalists' attitudes towards science failed to yield any strong anti-science bias. Indeed, as a group, the fundamentalists tended to hold quite strongly positive attitudes towards science. All suggested that science has improved the quality of modern life, especially if quality of life is measured in terms of greater convenience, improved transportation and communication, improved health and life expectancy, and the like. For them, science was frequently equated with its technological products, although several did distinguish between the search for basic knowledge and the technological application of scientific knowledge.

Individually, some of the respondents noted one or another cost associated with living in a scientific-technological society, but the overwhelming consensus was that the societal benefits of science greatly outweigh its costs. Personally, their experiences with science, while not extensive, were by and large positive.

- "Science opened up the world to me."
- "Science is wonderful. I don't have an anti-science view of the world at all."
- "Although science has made our life better, it's worse in some ways because we now have so many conveniences. We're too comfortable. But science is good. Science is good."
- "Science hasn't made people better, but it's made life more convenient."
- "Science has made life better in the physical realm. It has not helped us spiritually or emotionally."
- "Science is God's gift to man, to make man inspired to find the mysteries of the environment. Science allows man to appreciate God's world."

113

Most respondents had reasonable confidence in the information and judg-ments provided by scientists on such matters as nutrition, diet, medication, and environmental issues. Almost all said "Yes, in general" or "Yes, for the most part" when asked whether they had confidence in the information yielded by science, but several went on to specify areas in which their confi-dence was not so high. One acknowledged that "every once in a while" it was appropriate to question this information because human nature might lead scientists astray, especially where greed and politics might be involved. One respondent identified global warming and evolution as two politically tinged issues about which he is inclined to disagree with the scientific con-sensus. Another generally has confidence in science, saying, "I think they [scientists] do the best they can with what they have available," but believes that we would be better off if scientists used their spiritual side to help them find answers, instead of looking only at the physical side, which is all they believe in.

Most of the fundamentalist respondents seemed able to understand and accept the naturalness of public disagreements among scientists on matters of fact or inference (Example: Is global warming really taking place?), and were able to tolerate it easily. But all were aware of what, to them, was a higher source than science of truth about the world. One was able to accept the tentativeness of scientific information since only "time and history" serve to adjudicate differences in scientific opinion. The compelling issue for him, an issue that justifies science as a professional commitment, is that the urge to do science comes as a result of "God-given curiosity. If the Lord had not intended us to do science, He would not have made us so curious about the world we live in."

Another respondent, when confronted with public disagreement among scientists, reads everything about the issue he can get his hands on, "from right to left," and finally makes up his own mind. In addition he "took addi-tional courses [on controversial subjects] which might raise other points of view." The majority of religious fundamentalists we interviewed have rather high confidence in the information science offers and are quite accepting of disagreements. "Scientists, like anybody else, will have disagreements." But for some, "true science" will fit comfortably with what their religion teaches them about the world. "Our Maker has all of the say of what nature can do. Science is not unto itself. We need to recognize our Creator." Disagreements among scientists are acceptable because scientists are, after all, human like the rest of us. One respondent suggests that "these disagreements offer a point of reference for me that's both amusing and encouraging, and that is that things are relative. We really don't know everything yet, and the truth is, we're not going to know everything." This sense of humility in the face of human limitations and God's omnipotence seems to keep science, while a respected activity, in proper perspective. Disagreement, for one respondent, means simply that the search for truth is not ended. "When they disagree it means they need more information."

One respondent related scientific disagreement to his belief in and acceptance of Scripture as ultimate truth. "We don't know everything. Contradictions between science and the Bible arise because of misunderstanding of science, misunderstanding of the Bible, or the incompleteness of scientific explanations."

Had science, which most of them respect highly, either supported and reinforced or challenged and threatened any beliefs they were brought up to accept? For the entire group, the findings of science tended far more to support and reinforce than to challenge and threaten theological, moral, and ethical beliefs.

- "I get my values out of Scripture. As an entomologist I look at the amazing world of insects and I say, 'Thank you, Lord, for your creative powers.' Science changes, and scientific ideas which might have challenged my Scriptural beliefs have [themselves] changed so as not to offer challenges or threats. The Scriptural value of wonder at God's works is reinforced by scientific knowledge."
- "Science has supported what I grew up with and has not threatened or challenged any beliefs."
- "All science does is testify to the validity of my belief in a Creator. Science finds things, but who *made* them? There's a Creator out there who created everything."

One respondent chose not to attend a Bible college where "they're just going to tell me what I want to hear." Instead he sought challenges to his thinking in regular college classes and in his own reading. But ultimately, "truth can handle the challenges," and he found his values supported rather than threatened by science.

"Insofar as scientific theories can be *proven*, science generally reinforces my beliefs." This statement may refer to evolution theory, which the fundamentalist respondents unanimously characterize as "not proven."

Although science has normally reinforced his beliefs, he acknowledges that evolution "leaves questions," but does not shake his basic beliefs. In the final analysis, "I choose to look in the Book." There was a marked tendency to distinguish between *challenges* to belief that science presents, something many had experienced, and *threats*, which none confessed to having experienced.

In view of their positive attitudes toward science as an institution, do the fundamentalists believe most scientists are sensitive to the ethical issues raised by their work? Are they aware of accounts of scientific misconduct? What do they believe to be the cause(s) of misconduct?

Most respondents believe that most scientists are aware of ethical issues and adhere to ethical norms in their work. But a minority, while not asserting that scientists behave unethically, believe that ethics are largely irrelevant to most scientists. "Ethics are really not their point of view. Their point of view is expanding their knowledge cone." Similarly, "scientists are not generally ethical because their primary drive is for inventions and discoveries. That's what's important. That's the drive." "There are instances where results have been exaggerated from only a little positive data. If they are not careful, this could degenerate into unethical practices, especially with the pressure to publish and keep jobs and funding."

The majority, while believing most scientists to be ethical, have little knowledge of specific ethical breaches or cases of scientific misconduct. The cases of misconduct they have heard of are attributed to "overzealous pursuit of results," "big egos," and the competitive pressures of the scientific career.

The group of fundamentalists expresses a wide range of views on the set of issues falling under the rubric of science, technology, and the environment. While a modest majority accepts the position that "knowledge should serve mankind," and that, therefore, the primary goal of science should be to use and apply knowledge to achieve human ends, several are deeply concerned about the environmental impact of both science and technology. The primary goal of science, according to one respondent, should be "to seek to understand the natural world and modify it as little as possible to reach society's goals." Another says that "we live in a disposable world, and that's wrong thinking." This respondent, contrary to the position of the majority of fundamentalists that gradual lifestyle changes can effectively improve the environment, notes that "South Africa is treeless in many areas," and asserts that scientists must educate us to reforest and to prevent erosion. Further, this must be done in a fairly radical way. "While it's okay to take a tin can and recycle it back into another tin can, we need more basic lifestyle changes." Another grounds his strong environmental views in Scripture. "We need to recognize our Creator or we will destroy the earth. God lets man use this earth. We should apply knowledge about the natural world to introduce radical changes in lifestyle to save the environment before we destroy it."

Despite the expression of these strongly environmental views by a minority of fundamentalists, the consensus for this group of respondents is that scientists and technologists are creative and ingenious enough to handle environmental issues and manage natural resources in ways that will not demand draconian solutions, that gradualism is preferred because radical changes will not be accepted, and that scientific experts and concerned citizens should share the responsibilities of leadership in environmental preservation. Shared leadership is desirable because, while several respondents think scientists in general are probably sympathetic to the environmental movement, most believe that scientists are likely to be indifferent to environmental organizations and their concerns.

WOMEN AND SCIENCE

The views of this group of respondents on the issue of women in science cluster rather tightly. Almost all take the theologically grounded position that the Creator made men and women different from each other, and that as a result, we should expect different attitudes and different behavior from them. In terms of our questions, our respondents assert that male and female scientists will tend to choose different problems for study and will bring different perspectives to bear on scientific research. For this reason, most applaud the opening of science to more women. "Compassion and tolerance are more characteristic of women than of men. Men are more likely to grab the headlines and run." "More issues that are not male oriented will be researched, and that's good." "Women see things differently, not better or worse." Curiously, coming from a perspective 180 degrees from that of eco-feminists, their conclusions are strangely similar to those of these more radical feminist groups.

One member of the fundamentalist group, however, does not see that having more women in science will make much difference. Since "pure science is objective," the methods and approaches of men and women will be similar. "If you have a male mathematician and a female mathematician, what's the difference in their approach to solving a mathematical problem?" Another sees the social effects of increased numbers of women in science as more significant than the effects on science. While women have creative ideas and would contribute scientifically, "more women will no longer be in the home; child care will be delegated." Societal and household problems will be exacerbated as more women try to be productive scientists and care for home and children on limited energy.

The clear consensus of the fundamentalist group, however, is that increasing numbers of women are to be welcomed into the scientific professions. The differences they will naturally bring to task performance in science are viewed as positive; women are characterized as more tolerant, patient, compassionate, and sensitive than men, and these characteristics will motivate them to choose research problems men may ignore, and to bring to the task of research a desirable feminine perspective.

SCIENCE AND POLITICS

The group was asked three questions in the general area of science and politics. Has the advent of Big Science since World War II generally benefited society or not? Does the federal government have a responsibility to support and fund scientific research? What is their opinion about university research receiving substantial financial support from private corporations?

The responses to all three questions were remarkably uniform. Almost everyone agreed that Big Science has brought benefits to society, largely because it has permitted the conduct of research that would otherwise have been prohibitively expensive. This kind of research has helped "make our nation strong." "Teams of researchers working together have more insight and can do a better job of solving problems." But several noted that these benefits have exacted a price from society. Among the costs: When government gives funds for research it is likely that the results can be politicized. Politics can "force the hand of the scientist," and can increase the pressure on scientists. Despite the advantages of team research in Big Science, government funding can prejudice the results. Big Science has benefited society by providing adequate money and equipment and being able to get things done, but "it has been negative in terms of a colossal financial and manpower wastage."

In general, the fundamentalist respondents evince lukewarm support for federal support of research. A number acknowledge the necessity of such funding, especially in the areas of national defense and space exploration and where the welfare of citizens is involved. But almost all express some reservations. The federal government should not own or control results. It should not be able to "sit on" results and prevent their exploitation and use. Government should be carefully monitored so as not to receive a "blank check" for the funding of research. Government support has been helpful, but "it is dangerous to say that the universities 'deserve' federal research dollars." Government should support research but "we have no idea how the results will impact society."

Private corporate support for university research receives far more unqualified support from our fundamentalist respondents than does funding from the public sector.

- "It's beneficial to both the professors and the corporations."
- "Great! Corporations *should* be doing this in the interests of competition."
- "No problem . . . favorable."
- "Corporations tend to be more sensitive [than government] to issues about research and are more concerned with individuals."

But a few do express some degree of reservation. "To date, corporate funding of research has been handled well without a 'one hand washes the other' attitude, but there *is* a possibility of conflict of interest." Corporate funding involves vested interest, the profit motive, and exploitation, but that's not all bad because it stimulates competition. Corporate support is fine, as long as the corporations don't have a controlling interest in the results. Further, in some cases, like that of the tobacco companies, the research can be biased because the companies are looking for conclusions supportive of their interests. In general, however, federal research support is accepted grudgingly while corporate support, despite some risks of bias and special interests ("corporations don't do anything for nothing"), is embraced.

SCIENCE AND RELIGION

The final topic covered in our interviews involved relations between science and religion. The first and most general question posed explored the basic compatibility or incompatibility of religion and science. A majority of those interviewed maintained the compatibility of the two systems. One reason offered for the *apparent* incompatibility of the two was the failure of people in the two communities to be honest and to abandon the "sacred cows" that separate them. But the two are basically compatible because "faith can tell us what the senses cannot." Each has its appropriate realm and the two should flow naturally together. Since God gave us science to learn about the world, the two should complement each other. When they do not, however, it is the fault of the scientists, who "don't want to believe in the spiritual side. They only want to believe what they know is between their two ears. Each belief should inform the other, but scientists aren't willing to believe that." Another suggests that "true" scientific facts ultimately always agree with the Bible. A tension (between the two) is created, but illustrating, elucidating, and resolving it is part of the job of the minister. The answer to the question of ultimate compatibility is "Absolutely yes." "I have never found the two incompatible. They are not incompatible unless you make them that way."

There is, however, some dissent. One finds religion and science compatible on most issues, but on the issue of creationism and evolution the two are basically incompatible. "But that doesn't mean we should stop talking because, regardless of their opposed views on this subject, both science and religion are looking for a better world." Another respondent takes a stronger position. The two are basically incompatible because "science glorifies man and eliminates a Creator, whereas religion glorifies God. Religious people fear scientists because their beliefs threaten religious beliefs." But this view is distinctly a minority one; the general respect for science that permeates most of this group's responses to all of our questions apparently does not permit them to accept ultimate incompatibility of two systems of thought that have earned their respect.

The next question concerned past and present relationships between science and religion. Broadly speaking, which of the two was of greater importance in society in the past? Had this relationship changed in recent years?

The virtually unanimous conclusion, typically tinged with a tone of regret, was that religion's pre-eminent place in former times had been taken over by science in the present.

- "After World War II, science took a front seat. Science became God because science and scientists invent things we want and need."
- "Religion was more important in an earlier day. There is probably a polarization going on between very, very fundamentalist approaches to things and science currently."
- "I think there has been a wider pluralistic view; years ago, particularly here in America, the Bible was received with a greater reverence, and there's been a wider gap between those who feel that the Bible doesn't have any part with science and those who feel that science doesn't have any part with the Bible. . . . We have to create greater dialog and understanding between them."

One respondent saw a reaction against public-school approaches to teaching, especially the teaching of science, in the increasing popularity of home schooling. But the very existence of this reaction was evidence for the dominance of science in the contemporary world.

Clearly, the dominant view was one of regret that even though "there is religion everywhere, and though people may go to church on Sunday, that doesn't mean they have a relationship with Jesus. More people [today] are drawn to knowledge, which is more prevalent than in the past, and in that way, science has swung away and is more important today."

The responses to the next three questions can be summarized together, since they reflect a highly consistent set of attitudes. The questions were:

Should college and university professors have the freedom to introduce their religious opinions into the science curriculum?

Should professors have the freedom to introduce their religious opinions into classroom discussion of such subjects as human sexuality, family planning, and health?

Should elementary and secondary school teachers have the freedom to express their religious opinions in science and health classes, and when discussing such subjects as human sexuality and family planning?

With virtual unanimity, the fundamentalist respondents believe that college and university professors have the right—both moral and constitutional—to introduce their religious opinions into classroom discussions of science, health, family planning, and human sexuality. Only one dissenter says that "teachers shouldn't have the right to introduce religion into the classroom. Their religious opinions are their own and shouldn't be expressed." The implication here is that First Amendment guarantees against religious establishment are ultimately needed more to protect religion from government interference than to protect the public sector from religious interference, and that the introduction of religious speech into the classroom would ultimately be risky for religion.

All other respondents, however, view the introduction of professorial religious views in this context as not only a right, but an obligation. Perhaps the strongest statement of this view argues that "we have a constitution that says we have freedom of speech. Someone in the past has misinterpreted that. Let me tell you, any other religious opinion can be introduced in [public] school. They say religion's not in the schools? Well, let me tell you, it is! Just not ours. You can talk about any other kinds of religious beliefs and values, but say the word *Jesus* and you're in trouble. Only one religion is not allowed in the schools, and that's Christianity." At every level, introduction of religious values "needs to be done." "All other manner of beliefs and opinions are being expressed," and so the professors' and teachers' religious opinions deserve a chance to be expressed. "Secular schools incorporate values into their teaching too, so it's getting taught anyway." This respondent admits to a bias toward Christian schools, where religion can be overtly taught.

Other respondents agree with the principle of freedom to express religious opinions, but appear less vehement in their perception of the current state of religious expression in the schools and colleges. One says that, at the college level, professors are obligated to express their religious opinions because it's only "fair to students to let them know where they are coming from." Another says that "we do it [freely express our views] for everything else. It's healthy . . . but they [the professors] can't dominate. It's going to happen anyway." Still another says that "if you don't have that freedom, you don't have any rights. Scientists are supposed to better us, and should agree with the Bible."

Concern is expressed about the current situation, in which professors are at risk if they express their religious views. "If they do so, they are in a dangerous position, which shouldn't be the case. What are we afraid of? I mean truth is truth. And if his [the professor's] conclusions are faulty, it's good for them to be challenged and that's what the scientific community is supposed to do anyway."

Several repeat the theme, however, that the professor must avoid forcing his or her opinions or trying to indoctrinate the students. Professors should be able to share their religious beliefs in college or high school as long as they are not dogmatic and don't intend to proselytize. Whatever their religious backgrounds, it does affect their scientific views. They should be able to share them because they're important parts of who they are and how they teach.

Several respondents, however, have a different view on expression of religious opinions by teachers in elementary (and to some degree in secondary) schools. A few have no reservations ("Yes, religious views should be taught, and prayer should be there, too"), and some, while agreeing that the issue is "touchy" and "tricky," conclude anyway that teachers should have that right. Several, however, suggest that it's not the job of the public schools to teach values. This is an obligation of parents.

- "More caution is needed for elementary schools. I object to people pushing their religions on others [presumably younger others]."
- "No. At that level they should only share facts. Students at this age are not prepared to reason."
- "That takes on a different viewpoint. My own personal belief is that the parent in the home should have that opportunity, particularly in the elementary grades."

A final question dealt with the controversy over the teaching of "scientific creationism" and evolutionary theory in science classes at both secondary and collegiate levels. A large majority of respondents strongly support the teaching of both evolution and creationism, a practice which would permit students to make up their own minds. Most agree that both should be taught as "theories" that are not yet proven, though several expressed their own personal preference for creationism as an explanation of life on Earth.

- "Evolutionism should not be taught as a fact; neither should creationism. It's important to consider different views."
- "People need to hear both ways to determine for themselves what to believe. Presenting both teaches integrity for finding the truth."

None of the fundamentalist respondents takes—or even alludes to—the position taken by most biologists that only ideas accepted by the appropriate scientific community belong in the science class, and that creationism is not "science" according to this criterion. But one maintains that both creationism and evolution can become religions, and, as such, should be given equal treatment. One other respondent sees the issue as even more complex. Even though he is sympathetic to creationism, he views it as one of several different belief systems. If the schools present biblical creationism, would they not be obligated to teach creation according to the Hindu belief system as well as several others? On the other hand, "it is very difficult for the state to teach such a theory [evolution] as if it is without question. There are several theories on how life comes about."

Even in regard to evolutionary theory—the one issue on which our fundamentalist respondents are virtually unanimous in opposing a scientific consensus—their tone is not downright hostile. Rather, they approach the issue as one of equal time, of two competing ideas, both of which merit reasonable consideration. In view of the general acceptance by fundamentalists of biblical creationism as an article of faith, this reasonable and evenhanded tone may be no more than a strategy calculated to insinuate religious instruction into the schools through the backdoor. Even so, the attitude is a far cry from that expressed during the 1927 Scopes trial in Dayton, Tennessee, when William Jennings Bryan roused the local population to a fever pitch of hostility to the teaching of evolutionary theory in the schools. None of our respondents wished to excise evolutionary theory from the science curriculum. They wished merely to have creationism accorded equal treatment in the schools and colleges.

On the remainder of issues, the fundamentalist sample appears to harbor generally positive attitudes toward science as an intellectual activity as well as toward the practical products of science and technology. The fundamental rationale for this sympathetic view of science appears to be their acceptance of scientific curiosity as simply another manifestation of the will and the power of God. We are motivated to do science because the Creator designed us to be, and in turn, scientific observation and experimentation help us to see with heightened wonder and appreciation the world of phenomena created by God.

Interestingly, the view of science held by conservative religious groups is not even mentioned by Gross and Levitt. The index to *Higher Superstition* contains three references to the Institute for Creation Science, but there is no discussion of the goals of the institute, its criticism of evolutionary theory, or its view of science in general. The lack of attention to creationism by Gross and Levitt is perhaps understandable, given that their book focuses on "the academic left and its quarrels with science." But there is also an academic right that has its share of adherents to "creation science" and to the concept of a universe that was created in six days only a few thousand years ago. The current creationist movement in academe, however, differs markedly from the narrow, scripture-bound anti-evolution and anti-science activism that surfaced with the Scopes trial in 1927. Today's academic creationists are doctorate-holding scientists and engineers who use the language and the trappings of science to express their views and who are aligned with nationally powerful foundations as well as with prominent television evangelists.

Perhaps today's creationists are not viewed as so much of a threat by Gross and Levitt because all they seem to be asking for is "equal time" in elementary schools, high schools, and colleges to present creationism and evolution as competing "scientific" hypotheses. But given the broad base of popular support for creationism in the fundamentalist churches of the nation, the creationist agenda may, in the long run, constitute a more serious attack on science than anything coming from feminists or environmentalists.

Reflections of a Community Leader

> "It all started in the third grade. I was a singing frog in a musical at school—and I was hooked on music and theater from that point on."

My love of theater and music has always stayed with me. I took piano but never got to be very good at it, and I was in the school choir, the glee club in college, and the church choir. And that interest has stuck. My parents saw what was happening and they urged me to keep on with my interests. I was one of four kids, but I have a very strong recollection of my parents taking just me of all the children to see a touring company's production of Gilbert and Sullivan's *The Mikado*. Neither parent did much performing, but they certainly helped cultivate my interests in music and theater.

The community groups I've joined have been mostly artistic and musical, though I do belong to a lot of environmental organizations as well. I've always had interests in environmental quality and animal protection—that sort of thing. And I do take a real interest in the scientific aspect of environmental protection. But actually, I've had relatively little exposure to science. There was a science requirement at college, and because I'd had no chemistry or physics in high school I chose geology. The first semester was mostly the chemistry of rocks and earth—and that was okay—but the second semester was paleontology, and I thought that was wonderful. I could draw well enough to make good sketches of the trilobites and other fossils. But that's all the formal science I had, because I went from college into the Air Force and took no more science when I returned to college after three years.

I really don't know if there are areas of scientific research that should be prohibited territory. Like many people, I'm concerned about genetic engineering and how far that should go, but it seems to me that it's all right so far. But if, in the next hundred years, it gets to a point of guiding and controlling human development, I would have some reservations. But these reservations are not prompted, and I'm not hampered, by religious belief. For people who are guided by faith this may be a more serious problem. Of course, I don't see how it's possible that we're wise enough to calculate the future costs and benefits of the scientific research we do today. Some areas of research can be very threatening and frightening. But I think it's simply in our nature to explore and seek new knowledge, and there's nothing to be done about that. Sure, there are going to be disagreements among scientists. Usually there are good arguments on all sides of disputed issues. But the disagreements are typically resolved when science learns more about the issue. Then one view becomes generally accepted as the correct one.

It may be that scientific research would be a prominent part of my ideal society, but with my background I'd say experience with the arts is calculated to lead us to a better society. It might teach us how to get along with each other and make life decent for everybody—and life is certainly not decent for everybody as we sit here and talk. Interestingly, I do note that people who are professional physicists and mathematicians are pretty active in musical and artistic activities.

Of course, science makes it possible for us to have longer and healthier lives, but that brings its own problems. It makes it necessary to figure out how to give these longer-lived people enough money to live decently. In spite of the fact that science is involved in the competition between giant organizations for big money—look at the pharmaceutical industry—by and large I think science works for our benefit. In general, my understanding of science lends support to the beliefs and values I was brought up with, and I can't recall that science has ever seriously threatened or challenged the beliefs I hold dear.

Science is not easily adaptable to external control. It seems to me science propels itself, following the rules of its own logic, whether society approves or not. And even though there are bound to be flaws and misdirection in the progress of science, by and large I'm an optimist about the future. It would be great if science could help us stop killing each other and provide everyone with enough to eat and a decent place to live. It would be a wonderful world. But so far it's not done that. Something's wrong there. I do have reservations about those kinds of science and technology that attempt to alter nature very dramatically. Such attempts may work out for a while, but eventually they will put our environment in jeopardy. We simply must learn to live in greater harmony with nature.

I know some people are truly pessimistic. They have an apocalyptic view of the future. But I don't agree with that. Though I'm pretty old, I'd like to be around to see how things are going and how they're going to develop. I think sooner or later people are going to wake up to the facts of environmental degradation and over-population and find means to alter our course. I really do have that much confidence in our scientific and technological abilities. But this belief is rooted in my faith in human beings, not religious faith. Despite my early religious training, for most of my life religion has not been a shaping factor. And I think that for most mainline religious people there's no problem with incompatibility between religion and science. For fundamentalists who insist on a literal interpretation of the Bible—who insist on the literal truth and factual accuracy of the Bible—there is a real problem. And I'm afraid that, with the increasing visibility of the religious right, we're going to face more and more strident hostility to science.

I think people's attitudes toward science are certainly shaped by external events. In the 1950s, science was great and was going to lead us to the promised land. But then came the '60s and '70s, and Vietnam changed everybody's outlook. I think Vietnam was the greatest calamity in our country since the Civil War. Nothing's been the same since. Even so, I think there's a reservoir of good will toward science among the people. Maybe it's not as deep as it once was, but I certainly don't feel there's any general attitude of hostility.

I'm not as worried as some about support of university research by private industry or by government. There's justification for both. And I think most scientists are sufficiently ethical that they won't be bought by sponsors of research. Yes, I'm aware of occasional examples of scientific misconduct. But I think it's rare.

How does science know what it knows? It obviously uses reason and logic, observation and experimentation. But there's also some use of tradition and authority. And it may well be that there's something in scientific insight akin to revelation. I don't know whether Einstein suddenly had this great revelation or whether, through years of tough thinking, he just came to this powerful conclusion. But because of science's more organized dependence on reason and experiment, scientific minds are probably less likely to go off on some strange tangent—like all the flack about dead, white European males and all that stuff that we hear from some quarters. Makes me tired. And so, to that degree, scientific knowledge may be more reliable than knowledge gained otherwise.

I don't think that teachers at any level should voice their own religious beliefs as "truth." But it's impossible to teach about human civilization in social science or humanities courses without discussing the variety of religious beliefs held. You just can't understand human history without delving into religious beliefs. On the question of evolution and creationism, I guess it's politically correct for teachers to say that some people believe in the one and others in the other. But for a well-trained scientist, it must be a great temptation to say to the creationist, "Oh, you jerk." And inevitably, when you say some believe this and others believe that, some bright kid is going to say, "But teacher, which is right?"

Chapter 7

The Voice of the *Tertium Quid*

The tertium quid, literally the "third something," is a term commonly used to refer to a point of view or a body of opinion not readily aligned with either of two widely held and typically opposed views. When we selected our five key groups of respondents for this study, we looked specifically for interest groups with a stake in science or, at least, in science's implications for their agendas. The political left, for example, might be expected to have views of science different from and opposed to those of the political right. Similarly, the views of feminists, environmentalists, and religious fundamentalists about science are likely to be fairly unambiguously related to these groups' motivating and driving interests. As a counterbalance to these interested groups, we believed it necessary to identify a control group—a set of respondents—unrelated to any interest group having a stake in science or science's social, political, or religious implications. In other words, we needed a tertium quid.

Since we chose the respondents in the other five groups by identifying leaders or active members of local organizations with well-known social agendas, we followed the same procedure in recruiting the control group. Specifically, we chose people playing highly active or leadership roles in a variety of local artistic, cultural, or educational organizations—organizations on which the conduct and consequences of scientific research would appear to have no obvious impact. With the exception that its interests and activities have no discernible relationship to the findings of science, the control group was indistinguishable from the other five groups; its members' socio-economic and educational levels were comparable to those of the members of the other groups.

Similarly, the exposure of this group's members to science in high school and college was much like that of the members of the other groups. Most had taken courses in biology and chemistry or physics at both levels. In general they enjoyed studying science and did reasonably well in their science courses. Physics was least favored by a majority of this group, chiefly because of their limited mathematical abilities. Their science education was most useful to them as general background information and for the light it shed on the issues of daily living rather than for any specific instrumental or professional purposes.

Like the five experimental groups, this group was unanimous in judging that science has made life better, though "better" was defined principally in terms of improved medical care and living standards, two consequences of technology or science-based technology rather than of basic science. Two respondents suggested that, in addition to these material benefits, science has made life better by enlarging our understanding of the natural world and by teaching us to think more logically and rigorously. Only one respondent expressed any doubts. Science, she suggested, has certainly made life easier, but "easier" does not inevitably translate into "better." She speculated that society may have to shoulder some as-yet-not-fully-discernible costs as a counterweight to science's obvious benefits.

In general, this group evinced a relatively high level of confidence in the information produced by scientific investigation. But the initial positive tone of its responses to this question was, in several cases, followed immediately by a note of caution or even skepticism. For those who sounded this note, it was science's conclusions on environmental, nutritional, and medical issues that seemed most suspect. This skepticism was clearly grounded in the widely reported controversies and differences of scientific opinion in these complex areas of study. Despite this skeptical note, however, no members of the tertium quid were deeply disturbed or made cynical by the appearance of scientific disagreement.

- "Usually there's a sound basis for differing opinions."
- "Over time, these differences will be resolved by further scientific investigation."
- "Lots of areas of investigation are not that precise. There's room for disagreement. I like the fact that there's conflict. It encourages people to be open to new and different ideas."
- "Reasonable people can look at the same information and come up with different conclusions. The resultant discourse gets to the final truth."

Most of the members of this group viewed scientific disagreement as a positive spur for them to do more reading on the subject and to examine contending points of view more closely.

For the control group, exposure to science neither strongly supported nor seriously threatened beliefs and values they were brought up to accept. Several respondents felt that "in a general way" science reinforced belief systems in which they were reared, but none could readily cite specific beliefs or values. One suggested that conservation of resources was a value she had accepted and which science confirmed. Another offered good and balanced nutrition as such a value. But none dealt seriously with ethical, moral, or religious beliefs and positions. Most of the respondents in this group agreed that some earlier beliefs had been changed by their exposure to science, but most rejected the words "challenged" and "threatened" in favor of such terms as "modified" and "expanded." For none of them did the insights of science seem to produce a dramatic or traumatic rejection of or departure from beliefs held earlier. Rather, science "may have modified some of my beliefs" (without specification), "has expanded rather than threatened such beliefs," and "has caused me to question values," as in considering the issue of longevity versus quality of life, prompted by the ability of medical science to prolong life that she would consider of low quality. Two characterized their acceptance of evolutionary theory over the rather vague and ill-defined scriptural explanation of the appearance and differentiation of life forms that they had accepted earlier as a "change in beliefs," but neither found the change difficult or particularly disturbing. One asserted that choosing evolution over the creationism she had routinely accepted by virtue of growing up in a religious home "hasn't really been a problem for me."

THE ETHICS OF SCIENCE

The first and unanimous response of this group to the question of scientists' sensitivity to the ethical issues raised by their work was "Yes, they are." But for virtually every respondent, the automatic "yes" was followed almost immediately by reservations that translated a simple to a conditional "yes."

- "Yes . . . usually. But certain political issues can be involved. Even well-meaning people can sometimes fail to see things the way they really are."
- "Yes . . . most, but I'm sure there are some who are not."
- "Yes . . . but I don't know. . . . I think so. I pretty much trust people to be ethical, but I recognize that research is not always for altruistic purposes."
- "Yes, I think so. Maybe more so than the bureaucrats who drive the research with their funding."
- "Yes, but it depends on the science. . . . Biomedical researchers must think of the ultimate impacts of their work. A bridge designer has fewer opportunities to make ethical choices."

Despite the sensitivity of their antennae to the fine shadings involved in the ethical awareness of scientists, few in the control group could speak in specific terms about scientific misconduct or malpractice. Most had heard about the existence of scientific misconduct, and a majority of those who had associated it with clinical medical research, but none had much concrete information on the subject. One associated it with mistreatment of research animals; another with inadequate safety precautions taken by drug companies in disposing of possibly toxic wastes; a third with "shortcuts taken by some researchers"; a fourth with "subjecting patients to unnecessary and ineffective surgical procedures." None, however, was able to cite a specific case and most agreed that it was a rare occurrence. As to the causes of such misconduct, "greed," "expediency," "the search for research support and professional recognition," and "money" were cited.

Most respondents in the control group viewed both basic and applied research as important. But the consensus was that the search for understanding and knowledge of the natural world should be primary. The terms "modify" and "improve," when applied to the natural, appeared to give pause to several members of this group.

- "I have reservations about [research] goals that attempt to modify nature. . . . We must learn how to live with our environment."
- "In some cases, science can improve nature. But sometimes it's better not to tamper. We can protect species without trying to force the issue and really control nature."
- "Study of the natural world is primary. We have responsibilities not to intrude in the natural world."
- "We should not be trying to modify. It's presumptuous on our part to think we can affect something as massive as nature and to assume that we can change [nature's] total plan."

But constructive applications can be useful.

- "While learning is great, in the long run application for human benefit is significant."
- "Both understanding and application [are necessary]. Basic research is important, but so are applications."

For one respondent, the question of who makes decisions about applications of scientific knowledge was more important than whether or not such applications should be made. "The primary goal is to learn about nature and to share this information. But then we should let everyone participate in policy decisions about how this scientific knowledge should be used. Scientists should acquire and disseminate knowledge; the general public should formulate policy about how that knowledge is applied."

The tertium quid appears to favor gradual rather than radical measures to help preserve the natural environment. But the choice of gradualism is as much a practical matter as one of principle. In the words of one respondent, "radical change is simply not possible." Several envisioned the possibility of both gradual and radical changes, depending on the urgency of the specific issue, and suggested that the two approaches are not mutually exclusive. Still, it is the people who must "accept changes and participate in them. You can't mandate radical change" because gradualism is far more acceptable now to most people.

- "Gradualism and education are the way to get cooperation."

Much depends on where change takes you personally. "Talk is cheap; personal action is at the nitty-gritty level" and decides the directions to be taken by society.

It seems likely that differences in views of what constitutes leadership underlie the range of responses to the question of whether scientists or concerned citizens should provide leadership in the solution of environmental problems. A majority joined several of the experimental groups in asserting that leadership must come from both scientists and concerned citizens. A self-classified "middle-of-the-roader" says that "we need the knowledge and leadership of scientists [in understanding the environment], but we also need concerned citizens to identify specific problems and help promote solutions."

Another respondent says, "A combination of both. Scientists are doing the research. But the people must play an important role. When citizens are part of the discovery process, they will be much more willing to go along with conclusions and recommendations."

Still, a few members of this group did not take the middle-of-the-road approach. One maintained that "leadership must come from science. But this leadership must be based on scientific facts. Then concerned citizens must support these [fact-based] recommendations. There are lots of knowledgeable amateurs, but they are likely to be affected more by emotions than by facts."

On the other hand, one respondent maintained unequivocally that "definitely, leadership must come from concerned citizens."

There seemed, however, to be a general acceptance of the idea that if leadership means producing and disclosing the information on which action must be based, scientists are the leaders. If, on the other hand, leadership means taking action on the basis of this information, there will be no changes until concerned citizens make them.

Although a majority of the control group expresses lukewarm agreement with the belief that most scientists are sympathetic to a variety of environmental organizations, most are clearly uncomfortable with a generalization of this magnitude. One thinks that scientists in universities are somehow different from those working in the "real world" and are therefore less likely than their non-academic colleagues to see the "big" environmental picture. Several others maintain that "scientist" is a pretty broad category that undoubtedly contains both those sympathetic and unsympathetic to the agendas of environmental organizations. One thinks of scientists as generally in sympathy with the goals of environmental organizations, goals she characterizes as "unquestioned," but believes that the methods of some environmentalists might lead environmentally sympathetic scientists to think of them as "fanatics and kooks." Another thinks that since most scientists appear to be doing their research "for the benefit of mankind," their spirit of altruism might lead them to support environmental organizations since they, too, are acting in the interests of all human beings. Finally, one respondent draws a distinction between basic scientists, whom she views as likely to be sympathetic to environmental action groups, and applied scientists—"technical people" in her words—whose interests and agendas might lead them to be less sympathetic to environmental groups.

WOMEN AND SCIENCE

The implications of science being traditionally a largely male enterprise elicit remarkably little concern among members of the tertium quid, most of whom think that the methods of science involve little or no bias and are essentially gender-neutral.

- "Most issues that science deals with involve both males and females, so there's no great effect."
- "I hadn't really thought about it [gender bias in the selection of problems]. Probably there's some element of it in the selection of work, but I'm not very sure about that."
- "I have no personal data on the subject. I've read that male issues tend to be selected by male scientists . . . but there's not a strong bias. Only a modest influence on choice of problems."
- "No, I don't think so. The research goes along as knowledge opens up new avenues of research. The research follows its own logic. Gender is not relevant."
- "No. The only exception is medical research and women's health issues, which have been grossly under-funded. But in terms of general science, [there is] no distinct pattern of choice of topics. Pure science is not gender based. Really, it is the choice of sponsors—the federal government, for instance—that decides on topics for research."

When asked, as a corollary to the issue of the largely male cast of historical science, what the effects will be of the greatly increased female presence in science, the tertium quid's responses covered a relatively narrow range. Most, while not strongly committed to the idea that women do science differently from men, thought that certain widely accepted feminine characteristics "couldn't help but improve science."

- "If there has been narrowness [in science], the presence of women will broaden it. [This is] due to a difference in approach to life itself that women have."
- "I tend to think that women, because of their makeup, can bring better communication skills to science. They will be more inclusive rather than exclusive."
- "I hate stereotyping, like 'this is feminine, this is masculine.' Still, women may be more balanced, more caring."
- "There will be positive effects. Some environmental issues will be more fully explored. I think of women thinking more globally than men. This is a personal bias, but I think women think of the effects of what they do more than men do. Will women be more sensitive to ethical issues than men? Yes."

Despite these feelings, there was a strong undertone of not believing that the effects of having more women in science will be particularly striking.

- "I suppose it will open more topics [for research] but I really don't agree with that. I personally don't think there will be too much difference."
- "It probably won't affect science too much. Scientists will study the things they're interested in. We view men as more aggressive, but I'm not so sure. Lots of women are stronger and tougher and more aggressive than many men."

Several thought having more women in science would be good, but not necessarily because their contributions would be any different. It would simply increase the size of the pool of talent available to do research.

- "Women are as talented and able as men, but I don't think that [in doing research] they have particular interests that are gender based. Just because a person is female doesn't mean she's going to have a different perspective."
- "I'm all for women in science. It would be really beneficial now; we would be making better use of women's brain power."

In sum, this group unanimously supported the entry of more women into science, but at least as much for the reason of utilizing their talent and their research ability as for any major unique perspectives they will bring to the doing of science.

This view of women in science was strongly supported by their response to the direct question of whether there are distinctive gender differences in the approach to science. Typical answers:

- "Not really. Many times men and women will focus on different aspect of things, but there are not great differences."
- "Perhaps. But science has fairly fixed methods, so there's not a lot of give. The difference will be mostly in choice of problems rather than in the approach to doing research."
- "No, I don't think so."
- "They could be different. It is said that women are 'more intuitive.' But if we use standard scientific methods, I'm not sure that intuition plays that much of a role. This would be like saying that a woman judge would be more compassionate or understanding. This is not necessarily so, if they follow the law."

SCIENCE AND POLITICS

As in its responses to many other questions, the control group seems to cluster around a middle and moderate position in responding to the question of whether the Big Science of the past fifty years has or has not benefited society. Almost all members of the group agree that Big Science has brought some benefits. Among them: the provision of more resources for research; the increased understanding of complex issues when teams of specialists work together; the benefits of increased funding, both public and private; the availability of better research facilities; and the greater range of ideas resulting from collaborative research and the team approach.

On the other hand, the enlarged role of the federal government in sponsoring research may lead to extravagant costs and having taxpayers foot the bill for research they may not agree with. In the same way, while science and scientists have benefited from increased funding, there is an increased tendency to do particular kinds of research because a grant is available, not necessarily because the work will benefit society. Similarly, the dependence of science on the largesse of major public or private sponsors could prejudice the outcome of research. "We must be careful that the funding source does not control what the results or conclusions are, like tobacco industry–funded research."

Central to the issue of Big Science is the role of the federal government in supporting scientific research and development. Like some of the experimental groups, members of the control group expressed the thought that support implies control, since it is the supporting agencies that normally decide on areas of research that will be funded. Because of this possibility of increasing central control of research, respondents were asked whether the federal government should play a major role in funding university research. While our politically conservative group inclined strongly to answering the question with a resounding "No," and political liberals offered as strong a "Yes," the tertium quid tended to say, as it did in response to many other questions, "Yes, but." Only one member of this group responded with a flat "No," and only two offered a relatively unconditional "Yes." The others saw the issue in more subtle terms.

Despite a tone of mild reluctance, one respondent concluded that "in many areas, government is the only institution capable of supporting costly research: the environment, costly medical research, urban studies." Others said:

- "It depends on what kind of research. . . . 'Better mousetrap' research should be privately supported. But conquering AIDS [general welfare research] is in the public sector. There is not a real clear line between the two."
- "Yes. I would hope the federal government has some commitment to improving our lives. The government is 'we,' and we can't do much research on an individual basis. But government tends to have too many strings attached. In general, my answer is 'Yes' with some caveats."
- "Yes, public funding aids research. But we must take a hard look at research projects that will not serve the interest of the public as a whole. The smaller the population that will be served by the research, the harder it is to justify it."

As might be expected, the control group also favored the support of university research by private corporations. But once again, the endorsement of this practice does not come without reservations. Only two of this group gave unconditional support to this method of sponsorship. One said simply, "Not a problem. It's okay," and the other, "It's more appropriate than government sponsorship. Corporations usually have a goal in mind rather than simply spending a pool of money they've collected. R&D drives corporate sponsorship."

But all the others in this group approved with conditions or reservations. The following three responses accurately reflect the remainder of this group's feelings about the issue.

- "It's probably necessary from the university's viewpoint. But there's some concern over control of university research—ownership and rights. There must be clear prior agreement on rights."
- "It's okay, but universities *can* get in trouble with domination by corporations."
- "There can be ethical issues here. Who owns the rights to the finished products of the research? Does the private corporation benefit from university scientists' labors? . . . Using a publicly funded and maintained institution to benefit a private corporation?"

SCIENCE AND RELIGION

A comparable tone of ambivalence pervades the set of responses about science and religion. The dominant note is sounded in the answers to the question of the basic compatibility of science and religion. Most respondents felt that the two were generally compatible, implying some degree of incompatibility in specific matters. One said that the two were generally compatible, that there was no problem in his mind at reconciling the two and that both can fit together. A similar mindset yields the opposite response from another member of the group, who said that on the whole, the two were incompatible, but that this opinion probably reflects the fact that he is not deeply religious. He acknowledges that, among his friends, some mental adjustments have been made to reconcile the two.

- "It's easy to say 'incompatible.' But ultimately the two are compatible. Most important religious ideas are not in conflict with science."
- "It has to depend on the individual. Some specialized religious beliefs are incompatible with science. You accept what works in the context of your beliefs and values. It's an individual matter."
- "The two are compatible, if you are willing to make room in your life for both. If you use one to exclude the other, they're not compatible."
- "They are compatible because religious beliefs don't have to be taken literally. Literal religious beliefs can be incompatible with science, but this is not the way to take religious concepts."

These responses probably tell us more about the group's religious beliefs and practices than their beliefs about science. But there is a clear acceptance of science as valid and reliable information, and this creates a willingness to individualize and modify a body of religious convictions acceptable to them. If science demands flexibility of religious conviction, this group is willing to oblige.

While one or two members of this group think that religion has become more important than science in the last generation, a majority believes that science has become more dominant. Moreover, the ones who believe that religion has become more important and a more integral part of the community in the last generation think this has happened because religion has become less authoritarian and more willing to entertain and deal with questions posed by science.

One respondent sees greater visibility of religion, especially in the "strident criticism" of science by the religious right, but this does not translate into greater importance of religion in modern life. Another acknowledges the necessity of modifying traditional religious beliefs to accommodate such elements of science as the theory of evolution but clearly believes that progress is indicated by the willingness of people to modify their religious beliefs from a fundamentalist view to one that can include science's contributions to our knowledge and understanding.

While according to some, religion, in a simple sense, was more important a generation ago, it can retain its importance only if people are willing to permit it to adapt and adjust to science and not insist on rather more narrow and dogmatic religious faith.

Finally, the tertium quid appears less willing than some of the other groups to have teachers express their religious beliefs in science classes, although once again this conviction is hedged with reservations. One would deny teachers this freedom unless it is known in advance that this will be part of the curriculum. Another would forbid the expression of personal religious beliefs but feels it is impossible to ignore religion in any kind of intellectual history. A real problem exists when a fundamentalist student asks the teacher about creationism and evolution in biology class. Even though there's a temptation to say, "Oh, you jerk," the teacher must acknowledge more than one way of looking at the issue.

Another says "No" as a matter of general principle, but suggests that this is a very broad question and that responses tend to vary with the degree to which a critic agrees or disagrees with the beliefs expressed. In a kind of turnabout on First Amendment implications of this question, one respondent says that if a teacher's religious beliefs are going to bias his or her presentation of the course work, the students deserve to know what this bias is. A final respondent claims that teachers "are always" introducing their political beliefs into the classroom, and so there's no reason for them not to introduce their religious beliefs *if* they are represented as *their* beliefs and not as the Truth.

A similar response was made to the question of whether teachers might introduce their religious beliefs in classes dealing with such topics as health and human sexuality. There was a general feeling that such a practice is more acceptable at the college level than in elementary and secondary school. College students are better able to assess and evaluate teachers' views than are younger children. Even so, the general response was "No," once more with conditions and reservations. For one thing, approaches to sexuality, for example, strongly imply a contextual set of beliefs and values, frequently grounded in religious teaching. Without explaining the source of values underlying prescribed behavior, the class loses much of its meaning. And yet, there is a tendency to back away from the introduction of religious values in this sensitive area because of the range of religious beliefs represented in the typical classroom.

Despite the best efforts of teachers, however, religious issues may come up during student discussion of such issues as contraception, abortion, and sexual abstinence. The problem is trying to separate essentially inseparable religious and social values. One respondent concludes that there cannot be a definitive answer to this question, and that part of dealing with the dilemma is the skill of the teachers leading discussions. Another says it's all right for teachers to introduce their own religious values if, at the same time, they assume the responsibility of explaining other viewpoints.

One of the real difficulties, observes one respondent, is that, with the breakdown of family life, many children do not get values education in the home, so it falls to the schools to fill this vacuum. It's probably not desirable, in principle, to do too much of this sort of teaching in public schools, but it's also wrong to bury one's head in the sand and ignore children's needs. On the other hand, one of the stronger "No" advocates maintains that children are too impressionable to handle this sort of material in elementary and secondary schools, and that teachers should not usurp the parental role in teaching religious and moral values.

The clear consensus of the group is that, in principle, religious values should not enter the classroom (although it is somewhat more acceptable in college than in the lower grades, especially since attendance in such classes in the lower grades is mandatory). Still, most members of the group acknowledge that putting this principle into action is difficult and perplexing, and are willing to accept some values education if "it's done in the right way."

A final question dealt with teaching creationism and evolution as explanatory theories. A majority of the group concluded that it is not appropriate to teach creationism as science in science classes, though several could accept *some* treatment of the subject. One, for example, could endorse covering all bases by introducing all religious "stories" of creation, but was aware of the difficulty of doing this without one's own values coming through. Another would mention creationism as "a belief," although he anticipated that if evolution and creationism were offered as competing beliefs, any fairly bright child would ask, "Teacher, which is right?"

In general, this group's tolerance of ambiguity permitted them to introduce a variety of beliefs about creation and the origin of species, but their commitment to science would mandate a qualitative difference in presenting the arguments of evolution and creationism, with the one being presented as science's explanation and the other as a cultural belief.

The control group's responses to all the questions tend to portray them as a reasonable, non-dogmatic and open-minded assemblage, without a fixed agenda that dominates their thinking and their attitudes toward science. While many of them share the attitudes of the other groups in some areas, they show a very distinct tendency to see many sides of complex questions, and to qualify their answers to avoid inflexible, dogmatic stances.

Chapter 8

Interest Group Politics and General Cynicism

Group Comparisons

In this chapter we compare the general and specific views of science held by the six groups of science critics. We start with comparison of the topics discussed by the six groups in the preceding chapters, namely: general attitudes toward science, science and women, science and the environment, science and politics, and science and religion. Next we turn to comparison of group responses to questionnaire items about science on the topics mentioned above. This will permit us to see if the views expressed in semi-structured interviews are supported by responses to a questionnaire. Finally, we consider the views held by our six groups concerning a broad range of social institutions in the United States. These views involve confidence, or the lack thereof, in the professions, government agencies, and key social institutions. This will permit a determination of the relation between views of science and of other social institutions, and whether our six groups reveal a general cynicism toward institutions extending well beyond science.

GROUP COMPARISONS

In this section we compare and contrast the views of the six groups of respondents in five topical areas. The results of these comparisons are summarized in table 8.1. As an example of how to read table 8.1, look down the left-hand column of attitudes toward science to the third item under Science and Politics, "Approve of corporate funding of science." Reading horizontally, we find that feminists and environmentalists show a $-/+$ rating. This means that both groups had mixed responses, but they leaned slightly toward disapproval. The fundamentalists and the political right got ratings

Table 8.1 Criticism and Support for Science

	Feminists	Environmentalists	Fundamentalists	Political Left	Political Right	General Leaders
General Attitudes						
Science made life better	+/-	+/-	+	+/-	+	+
Confidence in scientific knowledge	-	+/-	+	+/-	-	+/-
Knowledge disputes are not a problem	+	+	+	+	+	+
Scientists are ethical	-	-	+	-	-	+/-
Women and Science						
Male science had negative effects	+	+/-	+	+	+/-	-
Women will improve science	+/-	-/+	+	+	+/-	+/-
Men and women scientists will differ	+	-	+	+/-	+/-	-
Environment and Science						
Pure/applied research	+/-	+/-	-/+	+/-	+/-	+/-
Scientists should lead	+/-	+/-	+/-	-	-	+/-
Radical change is needed	+/-	+/-	-/+	+/-	-	-/+
Science and Politics						
Approve of Big Science	-/+	+/-	+	+/-	+/-	+/-
Approve of federal funding of science	+/-	+	-/+	+	-	+/-
Approve of corporate funding of science	-/+	-/+	+	-	+	+/-
Science and Religion						
Science and religion generally compatible	+/-	+/-	+	+/-	+/-	+/-
Science more dominant recently	+	+	+	+	-/+	+
Approve of freedom of teachers to express their religious ideas	-	-	+	-	+	-/+
Approve of teaching both evolution and creationism	-/+	-	+	-	+	-/+

+ = most say yes
- = most say no
+/- = mixture, leaning toward yes
-/+ = mixture, leaning toward no

of +, indicating that a strong majority of these groups favored the practice. The political left, on the other hand, was rated −, showing strong disapproval on the part of this group. The general leaders group was rated with the fourth possibility, a +/−, indicating that its members gave a mixed response, but that they inclined somewhat more to a positive than a negative view of this practice. We start with a cluster of general attitudes reflecting confidence in science.

CONFIDENCE IN SCIENCE

Assessment of our respondents' general attitudes toward science and scientists is based on a sequence of questions directed at their confidence in scientific information, their beliefs about the ethics of scientists, and their opinions about how science has impacted the quality of life. These questions are directed at their general views of science, rather than specific topics such as women or religion, which would be linked to the interests of their group.

Respondents were asked first to discuss whether and how science had made life better or worse during their lifetimes. While the general emphasis across all six groups was on the advances in medical science, material goods, or computers, and how they had contributed to a better quality of life, there were some minority views worth noting. Feminists, environmentalists, and the political left offered comments on how science may have made life worse. Consider the following.

- "Science has produced many short-term benefits, but over the long term, life may not be better. Science has eroded the quality of life."
- "The better is that it has produced cures for illnesses, material goods, and things like computers. But it has poisoned the air, water, and food, and created a new kind of elitism—a technocratic class."

In contrast, the fundamentalists, political right, and the general sample saw mostly benefits from science. They see life as "easier and better" because of science, and only a small minority of fundamentalists seems concerned about life being "too good": "Although science has made our life better, it's worse in some ways because we have so many conveniences. We're too comfortable."

Although our six groups generally believe that science has made life better, they are more cautious and restrained when discussing how they respond to the information and judgments provided by scientists on such matters as diet and nutrition, medication, and environmental issues. The fundamentalists had the greatest confidence in what scientists say on these topics, and had somewhat diminishing confidence only in what they call "politically tinged issues such as global warming and evolution." They also express some concern that scientists fail to use their "spiritual side" in their work.

In contrast to the fundamentalists, each of the other groups has varying reservations about what scientists say on a variety of topics. Feminists exhibit the least confidence in the overall authority of science, followed closely by the political right. Their criticism is directed at the self-serving motives, the subjectivity, and the dogmatism of scientists. One feminist comment:

- "Depends on which scientists. There are a lot of very corrupted, self-interested scientists, and a lot of dedicated, honest scientists. I don't have overall confidence that they are either truthful or disinterested or committed to bettering human life. On a blanket basis they are pretty patriarchal about who does it and how it is done. And they don't understand the ways in which their scientific work is biased by their patriarchal assumptions. That's fairly general across the field, regardless of whether they are honest and dedicated or not."

The questioning of scientific authority by both feminists and the political right is filtered through issues that are central to their respective groups: for feminists, the patriarchal nature of science and how scientists deal with issues of human reproduction and women's health, and for the right, mistrust of government and bureaucrats who manipulate scientists through the research funding process.

The environmentalist group, the general sample, and the political left are more divided in their acceptance or rejection of the authority of scientists' information and judgments, basing their skepticism more on the nature of science itself, rather than the motives of scientists or the institutional context in which they work.

Virtually nobody was disturbed by disagreement among scientists on issues like global warming. Rather, such disagreements were viewed as part of the process by which valid knowledge is produced. Indeed, many see disagreement as highly desirable, as noted by one member of the general sample: "I like the fact that there's conflict. It encourages people to be open to new and different ideas."

All six groups criticize scientists most harshly for their insensitivity to the ethical implications of their work. By and large, scientists are viewed as driven by their own agendas of career advancement and research funding, unprepared to deal with ethical issues, and capable of rationalizing and justifying their pursuit of ethically questionable research. Many respondents assert that competitive pressures to publish and get research funds are so severe that scientists "have no time for ethical concerns." A less charitable respondent stated simply that "scientists can be bought." Only the fundamentalists have a majority believing that scientists are aware of ethical issues and adhere to ethical norms in their work. Even so, a minority of fundamentalists joins with other respondents in saying that "scientists are not generally ethical because their primary drive is for inventions and discoveries. That's what's important. That's the drive."

WOMEN AND SCIENCE

An initial question concerning women and science asked about the effect on choice of research topics of male domination of science during most of the nineteenth and twentieth centuries. A large majority of the feminists, fundamentalists, and political left believed that male scientists tended to ignore those areas of medical research that affect women. Failure to focus on breast cancer, alternatives to radical mastectomy, and male birth control are all attributed to a male bias. Male domination was claimed to direct greater attention to industrial technology and agribusiness technology, as well as space exploration and weapons research.

While the fundamentalists believe, as do feminists and the political left, that male-dominated science produces selective attention to certain topics, they attribute this to the theologically grounded position that the Creator made men and women different from each other, and that as a result, we should expect and accept different attitudes and behavior from them. The left and the feminists do not share this belief.

In contrast to the feminists, fundamentalists, and political left, the environmentalists, political right, and general sample are less inclined to believe that male domination of science produced significantly different science. The environmentalists note some effects of male domination, but the majority tend to see developments in science as somewhat independent of the gender of scientists, and they are not at all specific about the effects that are a consequence of male domination. And most of the political right believed that there was little or no effect of a predominantly male science. While one said that there was "only a minor impact on choice of topics," most agreed that "in general, the things scientists study are not gender specific." The general sample joins in this general chorus of believing that a male-dominated science did not significantly distort or bias the work of scientists.

- "Most issues that science deals with involve both males and females, so there's no great effect."
- "No, I don't think so. The research goes along as knowledge opens up new avenues of research. The research follows its own logic. Gender is not relevant."

A follow-up question concerned the probable effects of an increased presence of women in the scientific professions. Drawing once again on their theologically based view of men and women, fundamentalists see the infusion of women in science as welcome because women will *naturally* bring to task performance in science greater tolerance, patience, compassion, and sensitivity. These "feminine" qualities will motivate them to choose research problems men may ignore and to bring to the task of research a desirable feminine perspective.

At the other extreme, environmentalists are inclined to see continuity rather than change following from an increase of women scientists.

- "Other than the inclusion of women's diseases, I think that women scientists are interested in the same things as male scientists. They are scientists! So I don't see choice of topic being tremendously different in most areas."
- "I haven't been able to discern [any difference] yet. Maybe in medicine with more women doctors. I don't see any effects in chemistry or physics."
- "There will be a slightly different point of view, but the women are going to have the same aims as the men—job security, financial security for families."

The feminists, political left, political right, and general sample lie between the optimistic fundamentalists and the skeptical environmentalists in assessing the impact of more women going into science. While members of these three groups are generally positive about the benefits that will follow an increase in women scientists, a minority of each group says it will be "business as usual" despite the influx of women. This view tends to recognize that the new women scientists will still be working within settings where males will still occupy the most prestigious and powerful positions within each profession. "Just because someone is a woman doesn't mean that she will see the world any differently than the dominant society, which is based on a male perspective. She has to learn to see the world as a male in order to become a scientist."

A final question concerning women and science focused more specifically on male and female approaches to doing science. Did our respondents believe that women's approaches to scientific research will differ from those of male scientists? The large majority of feminists and fundamentalists said "Yes," but for very different reasons. Fundamentalists express a scripturally oriented interpretation of women as naturally more intuitive, gentler, and more compassionate, whereas feminists believe women will do science differently because of the way they are socialized. The feminists distance themselves from a biological account of why women scientists will make a difference. For example: "Do I believe that the presence of testes or ovaries leads to different ways of doing science? No, I do not." The fundamentalists are more likely to believe that women scientists will work differently than men because they are by nature and God's endowment different from men.

A substantial segment of the political right insisted that scientific methods are not amenable to change induced by the gender of the scientist, saying, "It would be condescending to think that women's approach to science would differ from men's." While the political left believes that women scientists will study different topics and will inject different values into science, as a group they emphasize welcoming women into science rather than specifying how they will make a difference.

At the other extreme from the feminists and fundamentalists are the environmentalists, who almost unanimously believe that science is science regardless of gender. They do not expect that women will conduct scientific work in a way different from men, and are inclined to think in terms of gender-free and universal methods. Closely aligned with the environmentalists are members of the general sample, who also express the view that male and female scientists will not differ in their approach.

NATURE, SCIENCE, AND CITIZENS

The first question we asked our respondents about science and the environment was designed to discover whether they see science as the pursuit of knowledge with minimal control over nature, or as the application of knowledge to modify nature for human ends. Of all the six groups, environmentalists take the strongest position that science should pursue knowledge without thinking about how to control nature and use it for human ends. Their choice of words bears strong resemblance to Jeremy Rifkin's criticism of science as a form of "controlling knowledge."[1]

- "I'm a basic scientist and I think we should know how the world works. We, as humans, are only a small part of how the whole thing works and it's detrimental to be anthropocentric about the use of science."
- "You're talking to a geologist who is very upset about man's modifying nature. It seems that every time we start messing around with Mother Nature we get into more trouble than we've been in before."

At the other extreme are the fundamentalists who accept the position that the primary goal of science should be to use and apply knowledge to achieve human ends. Between the environmentalists and the fundamentalists are the other groups who are either divided on the pure-applied question, or who take the position that it has to be somewhere in the middle. As one feminist put it, "There is emphasis on preserving the natural world, the environment. However, we have to be honest and recognize how we have benefited from the work of science. It has added to our comfort, our standard of living." This statement is supported by a member of the political left who asserted that "science should be applied so as to improve the human condition." Political conservatives are also divided, with half saying that "ideally, pure knowledge and applications of this knowledge should combine."

It is interesting that the general sample appears to share the concerns of the environmentalists when it comes to "modifying nature to serve human ends." Although they feel that both basic and applied research are important, their replies abound with statements like "We must learn to live with our environment"; "I have reservations about goals that attempt to modify nature"; and "We have responsibilities not to intrude in the natural world." The sensitivity of the general sample to such environmental issues may indicate that, of all the issues involving science and the public, it is environmental issues rather than women and science or religion and science that command attention in the public realm.

A second question asked whether science should choose radical (e.g., sharp reduction in auto transportation) or gradual (e.g., recycling) approaches to improving the environment. Environmentalists, feminists, and the political left respondents are divided, with some recommending radical change and some gradual or a combination of the two. Environmentalists clearly prefer radical change, but they are realists and choose gradual approaches because there is not political support for more draconian measures.

Fundamentalists, political conservatives, and the general sample are less equivocal on the question of radical or gradual change. They clearly prefer gradualism, because it implies voluntary change, while radical approaches suggest a strong and controlling role for government. A dominant theme was that more radical approaches would confer increased power on political entities that could ban and prohibit arbitrarily. Science was viewed as functioning in a political and economic context, with "environmental extremists peddling fear and terror to fulfill their political agendas."

The political conservatives continue to express their suspicion of scientists when they are asked about the role of scientists or concerned citizens in providing leadership in the solution of environmental problems, and they are joined by the political left in expressing a preference for leadership to be in the hands of citizens at the grassroots level. A repeated theme was that environmental leadership is fundamentally political in nature, and this being so, it should not be in the hands of an entrenched scientific elite.

Feminists, environmentalists, the general sample, and fundamentalists are also reluctant to see scientists in leadership roles. They are more likely to say that both scientists and citizens should be involved in providing leadership, but they prefer that citizens provide the leadership and scientists be the expert advisors. As one environmentalist put it, "The problem with scientists is that they tend to be apolitical. Citizens have a role because they can be involved politically. But the information must come from scientists."

SCIENCE AND POLITICS

A central issue in the realm of science and politics is the emerging and flowering in the post–World War II era of so-called Big Science. Respondents were asked whether the change from pre-war little science—science dominated by individual investigators working in small laboratories—to research done by large, well-financed teams of scientists has or has not benefited society. All groups acknowledged that some benefits have accrued to society from this change, but all, with varying degrees of vehemence, perceived some countervailing costs.

The religious fundamentalists were the most enthusiastic of the six groups about the advent of Big Science. Since "teams of researchers working together have more insight and can do a better job of solving problems, this kind of research has made our nation strong," according to a representative member of this group. The fundamentalists saw little to criticize in Big Science. At the other extreme, fully half of the feminist group expressed suspicion about the thrust and range of Big Scientific research, largely because these big projects tend to drain resources from smaller projects. An even more pointed criticism of Big Science was that most of this sort of research has been done for the military and that only a small share of it has been directed to "explicit human benefit."

The consensus of the other four groups fell between these positions. Typical of the mixed response was that of the environmentalist group, only one member of which maintained unequivocally that society has not benefited from Big Scientific endeavors. The inevitability of Big Science is suggested by one environmentalist's statement that "there's probably very little that can be done today by a person working alone, except for mathematicians and theoretical physicists, and even they need expensive computers."

But beyond this generally shared lukewarm support for Big Science, the political left and right diverged sharply on the question of the preferred source of support for this kind of research. The voice of the left was clear and unmistakable: If we are going to have supported and sponsored research in our universities, the source of that support should be government, which bears an overwhelming responsibility to provide research funds. While a few members of this group raised questions about military research in the university, public—that is, governmental—oversight and guidance of research was viewed as a necessity. But whereas the left generally saw state and science as acceptable bedfellows, they expressed almost unanimous rejection of corporate funding of university science, stating that "corporations corrupt science."

Conversely, the political right, while grudgingly conceding the necessity of governmental funding for some kinds of research, finds the government's role to be one of the big drawbacks to Big Science ("Government is not to be trusted"). The right opted, rather, for "a pluralistic, private environment" in which corporations provide funding for research.

The fundamentalist group shared some of the political right's suspicion of government, but chiefly on the grounds of waste and extravagance and fear of government's "sitting on" and owning or controlling research results.

The environmentalist group tended to believe that there is no real alternative to public funding, since "the government is us" and we have to decide how to spend our money for scientific research. "If science is to serve people for the betterment of life, the government has a responsibility to fund it." While the general group seemed to share this position, it typically said "Yes, but . . ." to both governmental and corporate research support. Leaving "better mousetrap" research to the private sector, government should chiefly provide support for socially desirable research for which no other funding is available.

Finally, although the feminist group greatly preferred governmental to corporate support of research, they, more than any other group, were suspicious of both government and corporations as research sponsors. While provision of research funding is clearly a responsibility of government, it may make government into too dominant a force. "It has gotten out of hand and influences too many other aspects of society, such as the university, in the wrong way." At the same time, public funding is far preferable to corporate, which is "very dangerous" because it tends to associate scientists with "the values of greed and power and prestige," and turns the university into a research branch of a particular company.

SCIENCE AND RELIGION

In view of a few highly visible historical episodes of antipathy between science and religion, like the forced recantation of Galileo and the Scopes trial in Tennessee, we first asked all respondents whether they thought science and religion are mutually compatible systems of thought and belief. While a majority of respondents in each of the six groups agreed that the two were compatible, there was a significant dissenting voice in most groups. Further, some of those who accepted the compatibility of the two did so for quite different reasons.

With one or two exceptions, all of the religious fundamentalists are strong believers in science-religion compatibility. Their typical line of reasoning was that since science is "God's gift to humans" to help them understand the world they inhabit, any true conclusions of science must ultimately agree with the Bible. Any apparent contradictions between science and religion are the result of incorrect or incomplete science that will ultimately be corrected and found to agree with Scripture.

The modest majority of environmentalists, feminists, and the general group who declare for compatibility do so, however, for at least two different reasons. First, their definition of religion is not necessarily grounded in "specific beliefs of specific religions" or in Scripture, as is the religion of the fundamentalists. Rather, they declare religion to be the full range of beliefs that sustain them and that inspire them with awe and a sense of spirituality.

A second reason for maintaining the compatibility (or better, the absence of incompatibility) between the two is not that they are felt to reinforce one another, but that they are two such different domains that they make no contact with one another and therefore cannot be incompatible. As one feminist puts it, "I tend to see them as separate explanatory domains."

The fundamentalists, on the other hand, find allies among members of the political right, whose attitude on the issue is summed up by one of their number who asserts that since God's moral law governs both the spiritual and material universes, there can be no incompatibility between good science and good theology.

Finally, the political left is a group that seems to have no truly dominant position on the issue. Their views range from a strongly accommodationist position to one voice that insists on incompatibility largely because religious beliefs "do more harm than good."

When asked whether science or religion has become more important in the last generation or two, all groups except for the political right choose science. Several, including the environmentalists, the political left, and the general group, appear to think this is a socially desirable development. One environmentalist, for example, says, "There was a time when religion told science what it could and couldn't do. . . . There are some religious groups that still try to do that. [But] science has broken out of those shackles and is not concerned about religious authority determining what it can and can't do." Another environmentalist opts for science, saying religion is a personal belief system that "is not going to put down pesticide use or clean up a river or see that we have an adequate food supply."

The religious fundamentalists agree that religion's pre-eminent position of a generation or two ago has been usurped by science but, unlike the environmentalists and the general group, they acknowledge this with a strong tone of regret. One says, "Even though [today] there is religion everywhere, and though people go to church on Sunday, that doesn't mean they have a relationship with Jesus. More people today are drawn to knowledge . . . and in that way science has swung away and is more important today."

The only group with a strong minority feeling about the increasing importance of religion is the political right. While there is some agreement with the other groups, several members of this group believe that a resurgence of religious belief and spirituality in the very recent past may signal a turning of the tide in favor of religion. One conservative sees a falling away from and a loss of influence of both institutions in favor of a "mindless anti-intellectualism."

On the question of the right of teachers to express their religious beliefs in classes in science, health, human sexuality, and family planning, the general group, the feminists, the environmentalists, and the political left face something of a dilemma. All are strongly committed to the ideal of freedom of expression and opposed to censorship in any form, and ask what the difference is between expressing religious beliefs and offering political or philosophical views. Yet all, with varying degrees of vehemence, feel a good deal of uneasiness about the practice and ask where the line can be drawn between expression, indoctrination, and coercion. All insist that any expression of religious beliefs be clearly and unambiguously characterized as no more than the teacher's opinion and all agree that such expression is far less appropriate in the elementary or secondary classroom than at the college or university level.

The political right believes that teachers should and indeed already do have that right, but most members of this group agree that no right is absolute. While they are far more comfortable than the feminists, environmentalists, the political left, and the general group with the expression of religious opinions in the classroom, they agree with these four groups that religious opinions must be clearly identified as such and not be presented, especially in the lower grades, as Truth. One objection to the practice mentioned in this group is the possibility of the usurpation of the parental right of inculcation of religious values.

The religious fundamentalists do not face the dilemma of trying to choose between the values of separation of church and state and freedom of expression. The consensus of this group is that teachers have not only the right but the obligation to express their religious beliefs. After all, "all manner of other beliefs are being expressed in the classroom," so why not religious beliefs? They make the claim that it is only fair to students to let them know where their teachers stand on matters of religious belief. Hence, they opt for open discussion of religion in the classroom and take serious issue with attempts to limit religious speech on constitutional grounds.

A final question involving science and religion dealt with the controversy surrounding the teaching of creationism in biology classes. The groups split three ways on this subject. Predictably, the fundamentalists strongly supported equal treatment of evolution and creationism on the substantive ground that both are unproven theories. Since evolution is a "theory" and not a "fact," creationism, as a plausible competing theory, deserves equal time in the classroom. No member of this group alluded to the widespread belief of scientists that only the ideas accepted by the scientific community qualify as "science," and that, therefore, science instruction should be limited to these ideas. Rather, they pictured themselves as principled, even-handed, and objective in proposing that all views be expressed and that students be given the opportunity to determine for themselves what to believe.

The fundamentalists were joined in this sentiment by the majority of members of the political right who, though less obviously committed to creationism as an explanatory theory, still supported the exposition of both views in the interest of fairness and because they value the individual freedom and responsibility of students to choose for themselves more than keeping science classes free of what one admitted was non-scientific material.

At the other extreme, the environmentalists and political left opposed the teaching of creationism virtually without exception and without qualification. One environmentalist said, "Philosophically, scientific creationism requires you to shut your brain off, and I'm dead set against that." Another added, "If it's a biology class, it should present biology."

In the middle, both the feminists and the general group expressed the personal conviction that creationism is not science and that it would be better if it were not presented, but did have some ambivalence about foreclosing any possible discussion of it. This left one feminist with the feeling that "I'm not satisfied with teaching just Darwinism and I'm not satisfied with teaching just creationism and I'm not satisfied with teaching them side-by-side [because they are not equivalent and comparable]. Best to let the Supreme Court be the final arbiter."

One fairly representative member of the general group took something of a middle position by being willing to introduce creationism as one of a number of "stories" of creation or as "a belief." But if both evolution and creationism were presented evenhandedly, it would not be long, said one member of the general group, before some bright student would ask the embarrassing question, "Teacher, which is right?"

GENERAL AND SPECIFIC ATTITUDES TOWARD SCIENCE: QUESTIONNAIRE RESPONSES

At the completion of interviews with the six groups of science critics each respondent was asked to consider nineteen statements about science and to indicate the extent of their agreement or disagreement with each statement. The nineteen statements can be grouped into six items reflecting general attitudes toward science (e.g., "Scientists sometimes pry into things that they really ought to stay out of"), three items on women and science (e.g., "Most scientific knowledge is biased because it has been done by white men on subjects that excluded women and minorities"), four items on human-environment relations (e.g., "Human beings have the right to modify the natural environment for one's own ends"), three items on science and government (e.g., "Much government support of science is, in reality, indirect subsidy of large private corporations"), and three items on science and religion (e.g., "Many of today's social problems can be traced to the erosion of religious beliefs by the findings of science").

Table 8.2 contains a summary of how the six groups responded to the five clusters of questions about science. The scores reported for each group are the mean scores of answers ranging from "strongly agree" to "strongly disagree" to the items in each cluster. The first panel in table 8.2 provides the mean score of responses to the six attitude statements about the effects of science on society. The higher the reported scores, the more that respondents agree with the stated attitude. Fundamentalists are most likely to agree with statements pointing to the negative effects of science, and the general sample is least likely to endorse this negative view.

The second panel in table 8.2 deals with questions indicating that science is biased against women because of their exclusion from scientific careers and from scientific studies. As would be expected, feminist respondents are most likely to agree with such statements, while the fundamentalists and political right are least likely to believe that science is biased against women.

Responses to questions about the environment and science indicate that feminists and environmentalists are most likely to endorse "living in harmony with nature," while the political right and fundamentalists are the least likely to endorse such views.

The environmentalists seem to stand alone in giving limited support for statements about limiting the influence of government on science. They are least likely to want to reduce federal funding for science. The general sample follows the environmentalists in a weak endorsement for reducing the influence of government. The remaining four groups provide generally similar responses, which indicate less support for a reduced role of government.

Finally, in the area of religion and science, the fundamentalists and the political right are most likely to endorse statements indicating that religion is more important than science. Feminists, environmentalists, and the political left are substantially different in their lack of endorsement for such views.

In general, responses to the structured questionnaire items are consistent with what people said in response to open-ended questions asked in the in-

Table 8.2 Attitudes toward Science (Higher mean scores indicate greater agreement)

	Feminists	Environmentalists	Fundamentalists	Political Left	Political Right	General Sample
Science has negative effects on society (R = 7 – 17)	13.2	12.9	14.1	12.5	12.9	11.5
Science biased against women (R = 5 – 10)	7.8	7.3	6.7	7.5	6.3	7.2
Live in harmony with nature (R = 6 – 16)	13.4	13.2	10.6	12.4	9.5	11.5
Reduce influence of government (R = 4 – 11)	7.4	5.2	7.3	7.6	7.8	6.3
Religion more important than science (R = 3 – 11)	3.9	4.1	8.5	4.2	7.7	5.5

terviews. Feminists' responses on the questionnaire indicate they hold the strongest belief that science is biased against women. Fundamentalists and feminists were most likely to endorse statements calling on humans to live in harmony with nature rather than to try to control nature. This is consistent with what was said in the interviews. Finally, fundamentalists and the political right provide the strongest endorsement of religion over science, which is quite consistent with what was said in the interview. One noteworthy discrepancy is found in the fundamentalists' strong endorsement on the questionnaire of items stating that science has had negative effects on society. These results are not consistent with the fundamentalists' strong endorsement of science and scientists in the interviews.

CONFIDENCE IN INSTITUTIONS

As another way of helping us decide whether the General Cynicism or the Interest Group Activism model best accounts for the various critiques of science, we asked our respondents to indicate their feelings of confidence in a number of major U.S. social institutions. A list of thirteen social institutions and professional groups was presented to respondents and they were asked if they had "a lot," "some," or "hardly any" confidence in each (see table 8.3). The purpose of using this list was to see if the respondents' views of science were systematically linked to opinions about a broader set of social institutions. Thus, we might assess whether or not there was a general cynicism loose in the land that might be responsible for the criticism of science.

The thirteen institutions about which confidence judgments were asked were the medical profession, the legal profession, religious leaders, scientists, Congress, labor unions, the presidency, the Supreme Court, major corporations, military leaders, engineers/technologists, journalists, and university professors. Arranging these thirteen opposite the six respondent groups yielded a seventy-eight cell matrix of responses. Of the seventy-eight cells, each of which indicates a respondent group's level of confidence in a single institution, fifty-three show a majority having "some confidence." An additional five cells show a majority having "a lot of confidence," while only twenty cells have a majority expressing "hardly any confidence" in a given institution.

If a pervasive spirit of cynicism were infecting our society, we would expect to see a widespread and relatively uniform distrust of all institutions by all respondent groups. But this is not what our interviewees' responses show. Rather, we see an overall normal distribution of confidence attitudes within which there are wide differences in confidence in specific institutions and in levels of confidence across the different institutions. This leads us to conclude that confidence in institutions is grounded, not in any general

Table 8.3 Confidence in Institutions
Percentage of Each Group Indicating "A Lot"/"Hardly Any"

Social Institution	General Sample	Environmentalists	Feminists	Fundamentalists	Political Left	Political Right
Medical Profession	40/10	44/0	12/0	71/0	12/0	55/0
Legal Profession	10/30	0/22	0/25	0/29	0/50	0/33
Religious Leaders	10/20	0/33	0/25	51/0	0/38	22/11
Scientists	30/0	67/0	12/0	29/0	25/0	33/0
Congress	0/50	0/56	0/38	0/14	0/75	0/56
Labor Unions	0/56	0/33	12/0	0/57	50/12	0/78
Presidency	10/30	0/12	0/0	0/29	0/50	0/67
Supreme Court	20/10	33/11	12/12	14/29	0/62	11/33
Major Corporations	0/20	0/56	0/88	0/0	0/88	0/0
Military Leaders	20/10	0/67	0/88	14/0	0/88	11/33
Engineers/Technologists	40/0	37/0	0/0	43/0	0/0	33/0
Journalists	0/50	0/22	0/62	0/29	0/12	0/56
University Professors	10/10	33/0	12/0	0/0	25/0	11/11

*The missing percent in each cell is for those who expressed "some confidence."

cynicism, but in the particular social goals and politics of the various interest groups. For example, the political left and the political right have the
highest levels of any group of "no confidence" across the most social institutions, although not necessarily the same institutions. The political left has
the harshest opinion of six institutions, including lawyers, Congress, the
presidency, corporations, the Supreme Court, and military leaders, while the
political right "dings" four institutions: Congress, labor unions, the presidency, and journalists (by harshest opinion we mean 50 percent or more
of the group says "hardly any confidence"). Neither of these two groups is
particularly positive about any institution with the exceptions that the political right has a lot of confidence in the medical profession, and the political
left a lot of confidence in labor unions.

Considering the responses of the other groups, environmentalists are
highly positive only about scientists and are critical of Congress, major corporations, and military leaders. Feminists do not express great confidence
in any group, but are very critical of only major corporations, journalists,
and military leaders. Fundamentalists have high confidence in the medical
profession and religious leaders, while they are highly critical of only labor
unions. The general sample does not express high confidence in any group,
but directs low confidence only toward Congress, labor unions, and journalists. None of the six groups is either very critical or very supportive of university professors or engineers/technologists, making them the "blandest"
of the thirteen social institutions.

Although scientists do not receive especially high confidence (except
among the environmentalists, who have a lot of confidence in science), no
one from any of the six groups expresses very low confidence in science. In
fact, scientists are the only group (closely followed by the medical profession) to be identified with "a lot" or "some" confidence. This pattern of
reactions to scientists fails to indicate any broad assault on science as alleged
by the science wars metaphor.

SUMMARY

In this chapter we made comparisons of the attitudes, beliefs, and feelings
about science expressed by feminists, environmentalists, fundamentalists,
the political left, the political right, and general leaders. A summary of these
views, presented in table 8.1, provides general support for the view that
each interest group tends to be most concerned about, and critical of, science in some areas but not in others. The areas of greatest concern or criticism are those where science impinges in the goals or activities of a particular group. The agendas of some interest groups, such as feminists, are broad,
leading them to be critical of science in several areas—women, environment,

government, and science. Other interest groups with narrower agendas, such as environmentalists or fundamentalists, reveal a pattern of criticism that is consistent with the Interest Group Activism hypothesis.

Group comparisons did not reveal the presence of a broad pattern of cynicism toward a wide range of social institutions extending far beyond science. Groups critical of science are not necessarily critical of most social institutions in the country. This provides additional support for the Interest Group Activism hypothesis.

Chapter 9

Reconsidering the Science Wars

At the start of this book we examined a wide range of views about science. Criticism of science can be traced to the origins of modern science in the middle of the seventeenth century. This early criticism, extending into the mid-nineteenth century, came from poets, artists, and philosophers whose concerns were not about the harm that science had inflicted, but were directed at the ambitious claims and prideful goals of science. These criticisms reflected a clash between the emerging age of science with the receding age of Romanticism.

The place of science in the world was greatly strengthened as its products, in the form of technological achievements, fueled the ambitions of economic, political, and military leaders. And the standing of science was especially strong in all sectors when it served unified national purposes, such as the two world wars and their aftermaths of international tension. The existence of broad societal support for science is particularly important because the costs of science, in terms of spending a nation's treasure and changing its traditional values, are actually and potentially very high.

However, when a society is no longer bound by the common goal of "defeating the Axis powers" or "winning the space race with the Russians" or "putting a man on the moon," questions are inevitably raised about the societal costs and benefits of placing science in so lofty a position of power and esteem. Several decades of escalated questioning of science—in the 1970s and 1980s—laid the foundation for what seemed to some to be the public eruption of the science wars in the 1990s. The critique of the misuses of science was perceived to have shifted into a more basic critique of science itself.

We have characterized the science wars as an alleged running battle between scientists who defend the achievements and authority of science, and an assortment of feminists, environmentalists, political radicals, and religious fundamentalists trying to topple science from its privileged perch by challenging the special authority of science and scientific knowledge. The

163

combative metaphor of the science wars has been featured on the programs of scientific meetings and scholarly societies, and splashed across the pages of leading national magazines and newspapers. The threat of the science wars has been depicted as nothing short of an all-out attack on the institution whose proven achievements underpin the extraordinary progress of the world's leading scientific and technological society. It has been represented that the deliberate rejection of reason embodied in these attacks on science not only threatens to dissuade the young from the serious study of science, but also opens the way for a return to the irrational thought that is characteristic of less advanced and sophisticated societies.

We have taken the combative metaphor seriously, and have sought to probe the attitudes, beliefs, and feelings about science held by leaders of those groups believed to be hostile toward science. By this method we intended to determine whether local leaders from feminist, environmentalist, and other organizations share the criticisms of science that appear to be widely expounded by their national spokespeople. We also hoped to learn about why people in a variety of groups hold their particular views of science.

An examination of the views of our sixty science "critics" permit us to answer several questions about the science wars that were raised at the outset of this book. The first question is whether science is truly under siege, in the sense that it is being attacked by many groups on a wide variety of fronts. This total war image would lead us to expect to find consistency in the criticisms of science that are expressed within each interest group and a significant degree of shared criticism across interest groups. This would mean that members of a particular interest group, say environmentalists, will be critical of science not only when discussing how science relates to the environment, but also with respect to its politics, its gender attitudes, and other subjects. And under the total war image we would expect to find that many of the interest groups will have critical views of science on a significant number of topics.

Simply put, the data obtained from our interviews do not support such a total war image. Each of the interest groups tends to be very critical of science in some areas but not in others. For example, environmentalists are most critical of science when discussing environmental concerns, but are not particularly critical when discussing women and science, or science and politics. Comparison across the interest groups also reveals notable differences in the criticisms directed at science. Environmentalists and feminists do not share the same concerns when discussing questions related to women and politics. The political left and right also differ in their general attitudes toward science and their concerns about the relation of science and politics, and about the inclusion of religion in science curricula in schools.

The interviews do indicate that there is substantial criticism of science coming from the members of our six groups, but it is clear that they do not speak with one voice that seeks to challenge and undermine science in all of its aspects and pursuits. The critics do not represent a monolithic critical voice, determined to discredit science's knowledge claims. Rather, what we hear from most of our groups is a recognition of the past contributions of science and a belief that science can play a very important role in achieving the things that each group values—cleaning up the environment, advancing equality, accepting religion as a partner, and reducing government and corporate control of science. They also say, however, that science and scientists should not have a blank check to do what they want without scrutiny. But this does not mean that any sort of unified anti-science movement is developing, or that irrational thought is being preferred as a substitute for science.

The second question raised at the beginning of this book seeks to explain the sources of criticism of science in U.S. society today. We discussed two possible explanations: General Cynicism and Interest Group Activism. The General Cynicism hypothesis states that criticism of science is a part of a broader criticism of a variety of dominant institutions. In this view, it is not that people are particularly hostile toward science, but rather that science happens to be associated with other institutions that are under attack, like Congress, the presidency, corporations, and the media, and therefore comes in for the same suspicion, skepticism, and criticism. The Interest Group Activism hypothesis, on the other hand, states that criticism of science is socially produced and that the means of production are the organized interest groups that shape the attitudes and beliefs of members in ways that are consistent with the goals and interests of each. Thus, people join political groups, environmental groups, or religious groups not because of their hostility toward science, but because of their interest in cleaning up the environment or furthering certain political or religious values. Once in these interest groups, they will be exposed to discussions and publications that indicate how science impinges upon their groups' agendas. In this view, members of interest groups will be most critical of science in areas related to group interests, and will be less concerned about or indifferent to matters outside of the scope of their group.

The results of our "Confidence in Institutions" questionnaire, presented and discussed in chapter 8, do not provide support for the General Cynicism hypothesis. There is no indication that our respondents' criticisms of a variety of institutions produce a spillover effect that is linked to their criticism of science. Indeed, a number of the interest groups that report having little confidence in a number of other institutions are nonetheless confident in science.

This leads us to suggest that the competing Interest Group Activism hypothesis is a better way of understanding why certain groups criticize science. We believe that the pattern of criticism of science summarized in chapter 8 indicates support for the idea that interest groups tend to evaluate science critically in areas most directly related to the goals of their group. This is especially apparent in the case of religious fundamentalists who express concern with a criticism of science primarily on religious issues, while being very supportive of science in matters involving women, the environment, and politics. The concerns of environmentalists also follow this pattern, in that the topics that generate most concern involve how science impinges on the environment, how to prevent private corporations (but not government) from funding research, and how creation science should be rejected as a legitimate topic for inclusion in science courses. But environmentalists are not especially concerned about science and women's issues, about Big Science, or government support of science. The feminist respondents, however, do not quite fit the more selective pattern exhibited by fundamentalists or environmentalists, since they are critical of science on matters related to the environment, politics, and religion as well as those involving women. In short, their critical lens is much wider because the ideology of their group embraces a larger number of concerns. Feminists are drawn into issues of the environment through eco-feminism and are drawn into religious issues through their concern about the religious roots of patriarchy.

The political left tends to view science through its primary concern with corporate power and capitalism, while the political right is focused on how the power of government limits the freedom of the individual. Although the left and right differ in their specific criticisms of science, what they have in common is a view that science has been co-opted, perverted, or captured by the undue influence of the dominant institution of their choice. Both groups assess and criticize science through their own ideological lens.

The general sample is not particularly concerned about or critical of science in any of the areas of discussion. While the leaders from this sector of the community are aware of many of the issues involving science, they do not discuss these issues with the aid of a particular group interest or ideological perspective. Thus, their response to science is also consistent with the Interest Group Activism hypothesis.

The local feminists, environmentalists, and political and religious activists share with their national leaders a general view that science, as an institution in U.S. society, is in trouble. Science's problems, however, do not stem from the critics' attacks, but from failures within the scientific community. Two points are mentioned with some frequency by local critics as the reasons for the loss of public trust in science. First is the failure of self-regulation to prevent a variety of scientific misconduct such as misuse of funds, falsification of findings, and fraud. The second problem, which is linked to the first, concerns the dependence of modern science on external funding from government and, increasingly, corporations. The dependence leads to extreme competition among scientists, and the inevitable shortcuts to get an edge in the race for funds. The growing importance of corporate funding for individual scientists (government funding for the political right and fundamentalists) and the encouragement of industry-university collaboration has led many critics, and the public at large, to see science as just another special interest group. The products of science, in the form of useful knowledge, had once been thought of as public knowledge, but increasingly today such knowledge is bought to serve private interests.

Some national analysts of science, such as Dorothy Nelkin, have noted the unwillingness of science's defenders to acknowledge the above noted problems.

> Thus, in defending their discipline against critical public attitudes, scientists are arguing with extraordinary passion to support their own dispassionate objectivity. They want once again to be perceived as pure, unsullied seekers after truth, and they want to define their own history and contemporary practice in just such terms.[1]

One final word: In their literature, the defenders of science reserve perhaps their bitterest criticism for members of what they call "the academic left," the post-modern social scientists and humanists who, in the last twenty years or so, have written numerous analyses of science that attempt to demystify it and to demonstrate its subjectivity, its contextuality, and its rhetorical characteristics. In their dethroning of scientific positivism, these critics have tried to portray scientific knowledge as fundamentally no more than a social construct that does not deserve any especially privileged status.

As we launched this study, we anticipated that many of our respondents would bring up these characterizations of science, especially when we encouraged them to discuss public scientific controversy, scientific ethics, and their confidence in the information provided by scientists. However, *not one* respondent brought up any of the issues related to social constructivism even though interviews were being done at the same time that wide media coverage was being given to physicist Alan Sokal's hoax article published in 1996 in the post-modern journal *Social Text*, and even though a number of respondents are professionally active as scientists. This leads us to conclude that, despite the concerns of science's spokespeople, the battle over social constructivism is a minor in-house academic quarrel with essentially no public following and is likely to have little impact on public understanding, public appreciation, or public funding of science.

It has also been noted by critics of science that many of the critiques that flowed from the social studies "of 'proof,' of 'truth' and 'rationality,' even of 'objectivity'—rested critically not on the abandonment of these values, but rather on their deployment in forms of analysis in which scientists themselves were neither expert, nor to which, for the most part, they were even privy."[2]

The results of this case study confirm, at the most general level, the proposition that knowledge is socially situated. Combatants in the science wars are equipped with ideological commitments that shape the questions they ask and the answers they construct. Science's defenders remain strongly wedded to the power of their special expertise, which provides an intensity of experience that can easily ignore the human dimensions of their work. Experts are trained to believe in the objective, non-political nature of their knowledge claims, and to be suspicious of those who would criticize those claims without the benefit of that same expertise. On the other side of this contested terrain are the critics of science who are equipped with value commitments that call for change in the institutional arrangements that sustain and direct science. The critics of science in this study do not provide a strong challenge to the *content* of science viewed as truths, but they do deny that those truths are the product of knowledge creation by non-political, objective experts. The value commitments of the critics lead them to assess science in terms of the contributions made to a more just and humane social order.

Does this mean that everything is driven by ideology, and that all knowledge is ideological and therefore particular and relative? We think not! Science defenders obviously believe in objectivity and truth. Critics of science, with the exception of some post-modernists, also believe in the possibility of objectivity and truth. What may be emerging in this contentious debate about how knowledge is produced and used is a recognition that truth will have to be negotiated by an expanded pool of consequential actors with the right to speak. "Experts" from the professions and academic disciplines and political and economic elites will be joined by groups representing other interests and values to collectively shape the production and use of knowledge relevant to the larger society. A combination of cognitive and value judgments will be needed to deal with real-world problems, and knowledge will be socially and democratically situated.

Endnotes

CHAPTER 1

1. Dixy Lee Ray, "Who's to Blame When the Public Misunderstands Science?" *The Scientist* (April 16, 1990), 17.

2. Jonathan Swift, *Gulliver's Travels*, ed. Colin McKelvie (Belfast: Appletree, 1976).

3. John Adolphous Etzler, *The Paradise Within the Reach of All Men, Without Labor, by Powers of Nature and Machinery: An Address to All Intelligent Men*, second English edition (London: J. Cleave, 1842).

4. Henry David Thoreau, *Miscellanies* (Boston: Houghton Mifflin, 1895).

5. Walt Whitman, "When I Heard the Learn'd Astronomer," in *Leaves of Grass* (New York: The Limited Editions Club, 1929).

6. John Ziman, *Public Knowledge: The Social Dimensions of Science* (Cambridge: Oxford University Press, 1968), 23.

7. Thomas Kuhn, *The Structure of Scientific Revolutions* (Chicago: University of Chicago Press, 1970).

8. Kuhn, *The Structure of Scientific Revolutions*, 6.

9. Barry Barnes and Steven Shapin, eds., *Natural Order* (Beverly Hills: Sage, 1979), 9.

10. Harry Collins and Trevor Pinch, *The Golem* (Cambridge: Oxford University Press, 1993), 142.

11. Robert Merton, *Social Research and the Practicing Professions* (Cambridge, Mass.: Abt Books, 1982).

12. William Broad and Nicholas Wade, *Betrayers of the Truth* (New York: Simon & Schuster, 1982).

13. Bobbie Jo Gottschalk, "Cold Fusion: A Descriptive Case Study" (master's thesis, Purdue University, 1991).

14. James H. Jones, *Bad Blood: The Tuskegee Syphilis Experiment* (New York: Free Press, 1983).

15. Philip J. Hilts, "Experiments on Children Are Reviewed," New York Times, April 18 1998, B3:6.

16. Rachel Carson, *Silent Spring* (Boston: Houghton Mifflin, 1962).

17. Lynn White Jr., *Machina ex Deo: Essays on the Dynamism of Western Culture* (Cambridge, Mass.: MIT Press, 1968).

18. Daryl E. Chubin and Edward J. Hackett, *Peerless Science* (Albany: SUNY Press, 1990), 11.

19. John C. Whitcomb and Henry M. Morris, *The Genesis Flood* (Ada, Mich.: Baker Books, 1969).

20. Duane Gish, *Evolution: The Challenge of the Fossil Record* (El Cajon, Calif.: Creation Life Publishers, Master Books Division, 1985).

21. Phillip E. Johnson, *Darwin on Trial* (Washington, D.C.: Regnery Publishing, 1991).

22. Paul R. Gross and Norman Levitt, *Higher Superstition: The Academic Left and Its Quarrels with Science* (Baltimore, Md.: Johns Hopkins University Press, 1994).

23. Alan Sokal, "Transgressing the Boundaries: The Transformative Hermeneutics of Quantum Gravity," *Social Text* 47/48 (Spring/Summer 1996), 217–52.

24. Alan Sokal, "A Physicist Experiments with Cultural Studies," *Lingua Franca* 6 (May/June 1996), 62–64.

25. Henry Greenberg, "Introductory Remarks: Medicine Took an Earlier Flight," in *The Flight from Science and Reason*, ed. Paul R. Gross, Norman Levitt, and Martin W. Lewis (New York: New York Academy of Sciences, 1996), ix.

26. Mario Bunge, "In Praise of Intolerance to Charlatanism in Academia," in *The Flight*, ed. Gross, Levitt, and Lewis, 110.

27. Andrew Ross, "Introduction," in *Science Wars*, ed. Andrew Ross (Durham, N.C.: Duke University Press, 1996), 11.

28. Carolyn C. Perrucci, Robert Perrucci, Dena B. Targ, and Harry Targ, *Plant Closings: International Context and Social Costs* (New York: Aldine de Gruyter, 1988).

CHAPTER 2

1. Quoted in Gerald Holton, *Science and Anti-Science* (Cambridge, Mass.: Harvard University Press, 1993), 168.

2. Janny Scott, "An Intimate Story Is Told at Last, by the Survivor," *New York Times*, May 7, 1998, B1.

3. Sandra Harding, *The Science Question in Feminism* (Ithaca, N.Y.: Cornell University Press, 1986).

4. Harding, *The Science Question in Feminism*, 23.

5. Paul R. Gross and Norman Levitt, *Higher Superstition: The Academic Left and Its Quarrels with Science* (Baltimore, Md.: Johns Hopkins University Press, 1994), 108.

CHAPTER 3

1. Paul R. Gross and Norman Levitt, *Higher Superstition: The Academic Left and Its Quarrels with Science* (Baltimore, Md.: Johns Hopkins University Press, 1994), 157.

2. Carolyn Merchant, *Radical Ecology: The Search for a Livable World* (New York: Routledge, 1992), 239.

3. Jeremy Rifkin, *Declaration of a Heretic* (London: Routledge & Kegan Paul, 1985), 83.

4. Rifkin, *Declaration of a Heretic,* 90.

5. Gross and Levitt, *Higher Superstition,* 163.

6. Gross and Levitt, *Higher Superstition,* 152–53.

7. Gross and Levitt, *Higher Superstition,* 237.

CHAPTER 4

1. Norman Levitt, *Technoscience: Newsletter of the Society for Social Studies of Science* 9 (Winter 1996), 18.

CHAPTER 8

1. Jeremy Rifkin, *Declaration of a Heretic* (London: Routledge & Kegan Paul), 83.

CHAPTER 9

1. Dorothy Nelkin, "The Science Wars: Responses to a Marriage Failed," in *Science Wars,* ed. Andrew Ross (Durham, N.C.: Duke University Press), 120.

2. Evelyn Fox Keller, "Science and Its Critics," *Academe* 81 (September–October 1995), 13.

Bibliography

Barnes, Barry, David Bloor, and John Henry. *Scientific Knowledge: A Sociological Analysis.* Chicago: University of Chicago Press, 1996.

Barnes, Barry, and Steven Shapin, eds. *Natural Order.* Beverly Hills: Sage, 1979.

Broad, William, and Nicholas Wade. *Betrayers of the Truth.* New York: Simon & Schuster, 1982.

Chubin, Daryl E., and Ellen W. Chu, eds. *Science Off the Pedestal.* Belmont, Calif.: Wadsworth, 1989.

Chubin, Daryl E., and Edward Hackett. *Peerless Science.* Albany: SUNY Press, 1990.

Collins, Harry, and Trevor Pinch. *The Golem.* Cambridge, Mass.: Oxford University Press, 1993.

Darlington, C.D. *The Conflict of Science and Society.* London: Watts & Co., 1948.

Etzler, John Adolphous. *The Paradise Within the Reach of All Men, Without Labor, by Powers of Nature and Machinery: An Address to All Intelligent Men,* second English edition. London: J. Cleave, 1842.

Feyerabend, Paul. *Science in a Free Society.* London: Verso, 1982.

Futuyma, Douglas. *Science on Trial.* New York: Pantheon, 1983.

Gieryn, Tom. "Policing STS: A Boundary Work Souvenir from the Smithsonian Exhibition on 'Science in American Life.' " Science, Technology and Human Values 21:100–115, 1996.

Gish, Duane. *Evolution: The Challenge of the Fossil Record.* El Cajon, Calif.: Creation Life Publishers, Master Books Division, 1985.

Grinnell, Frederick. *The Scientific Attitude,* second edition. New York: Guilford, 1992.

Gross, Alan G. *The Rhetoric of Science.* Cambridge, Mass.: Harvard University Press, 1990.

Gross, Paul R., and Norman Levitt. *Higher Superstition: The Academic Left and Its Quarrels with Science.* Baltimore, Md.: Johns Hopkins University Press, 1994.

Gross, Paul R., Norman Levitt, and Martin W. Lewis, eds. *The Flight from Science and Reason.* New York: New York Academy of Sciences, 1996.

Gross, Paul. "Reply to Tom Gieryn." Science, Technology and Human Values 21:116–20, 1996.

Harding, Sandra. "Science is 'Good to Think With,' " in Science Wars, ed. Andrew Ross. Durham, N.C.: Duke University Press, 1996.

Harding, Sandra. *Whose Science? Whose Knowledge?* Ithaca, N.Y.: Cornell University Press, 1991.

Holton, Gerald. *Science and Anti-Science.* Cambridge, Mass.: Harvard University Press, 1993.

Hubbard, Ruth. "Gender and Genitals: Constructs of Sex and Gender," in *Science Wars,* ed. Andrew Ross. Durham, N.C.: Duke University Press, 1996.

Johnson, Phillip. "What (If Anything) Hath God Wrought? Academic Freedom and the Religious Professor." *Academe* 81, September–October:16–20, 1995.

Jones, James H. *Bad Blood: The Tuskeegee Syphilis Experiment.* New York: Free Press, 1983.

Keller, Evelyn Fox. "Science and Its Critics." *Academe* 81, September–October:10–15, 1995.

Knorr-Cetina, K.D., and M. Mulkay, eds. *Science Observed: Perspectives on the Social Study of Science.* London: Sage, 1983.

Kuhn, Thomas S. *The Structure of Scientific Revolutions.* Chicago: University of Chicago Press, 1970.

Latour, Bruno, and Steve Woolgar. *Laboratory Life: The Construction of Scientific Facts.* Princeton, N.J.: Princeton University Press, 1986.

McMullin, Ernan, ed. *The Social Dimensions of Science.* South Bend, Ind.: University of Notre Dame Press, 1992.

Merchant, Carolyn. *Radical Ecology: The Search for a Livable World.* New York: Routledge, 1992.

Merton, Robert K. *Social Research and the Practicing Professions.* Cambridge, Mass.: Abt Books, 1982.

Nelkin, Dorothy. "The Science Wars: Responses to a Marriage Failed," in *Science Wars,* ed. Andrew Ross. Durham, N.C.: Duke University Press, 1996.

Perrucci, Carolyn C., Robert Perrucci, Dena B. Targ, and Harry R. Targ. *Plant Closings: International Context and Social Costs.* New York: Aldine de Gruyter, 1988.

Price, Derek de Solla. *Little Science, Big Science.* New York: Columbia University Press, 1986.

Ray, Dixy Lee. "Who's to Blame When the Public Misunderstands Science?" *The Scientist,* April 16:17–20, 1990.

Restivo, Sal. "Critical Sociology of Science," in *Science on the Pedestal,* ed. Darly E. Chubin and Ellen W. Chu. Belmont, Calif.: Wadsworth, 1989.

Rifkin, Jeremy. *Declaration of a Heretic.* London: Routledge & Kegan Paul, 1985.

Ross, Andrew, ed. *Science Wars.* Durham, N.C.: Duke University Press, 1996.

Roszak, Theodore. *The Making of a Counter Culture.* Garden City, N.Y.: Anchor, 1969.

Ruse, Michael. *Mystery of Mysteries: Is Evolution a Social Construction?* Cambridge, Mass.: Harvard University Press, 1999.

Ruse, Michael. *But Is It Science?* Buffalo, N.Y.: Prometheus, 1988.

Ruse, Michael. "Naturalistic Fallacy." *Reason,* October:53–58, 1996.

Sokal, Alan. "A Physicist Experiments with Cultural Studies." *Lingua Franca* 6, May/June: 62–64, 1996.

Webster, Andrew. *Science, Technology and Society.* New Brunswick, N.J.: Rutgers University Press, 1991.

Winner, Langdon. "The Gloves Come Off: Shattered Alliances in Science and Technology Studies," in *Science Wars,* ed. Andrew Ross. Durham, N.C.: Duke University Press, 1996.

Ziman, John. *Public Knowledge.* Cambridge: Oxford University Press, 1968.

Index

About the Authors

Leon E. Trachtman is emeritus professor of communication and former chair of the Interdisciplinary Science and Culture Committee at Purdue University. After completing his graduate work at Johns Hopkins University he taught at Hood College and was a science writer and editor at the National Institutes of Health. At Purdue since 1958, he has been the recipient of grants from the National Science Foundation and the National Endowment for the Humanities for the design of seminars in science and culture and for the study of professional whistleblowing. He is co-author of *Divided Loyalties*, a study of whistleblowing at BART, and served as general editor of the Science, Technology and Human Values series of the Purdue University Press. He has published widely in such journals as *Science, Technology and Human Values, Politics and the Life Sciences, Social Problems,* and the *Bulletin of Science, Technology and Society.*

Robert Perrucci is professor of sociology at Purdue University. He is the author of over seventy journal articles and book chapters and the author or editor of fourteen books. His most recent book (with Earl Wysong) is *The New Class Society*, an examination of the changing structure of class inequality in the United States. He has served as the editor of *The American Sociologist* and *Social Problems* and has been selected by the American Sociological Association to be co-editor, with Jo Ann Miller, of *Contemporary Sociology*, the second largest circulation sociology journal in the world. He is also president of the Society for the Study of Social Problems. His current project takes him to the border of fact and fiction as he and Melissa Marcello write *Democracy for Dummies: America's Secret Plan for World Domination.*

Michael Dennis, a Ph.D. candidate at Purdue University, is a lecturer in communication at the University of Kansas, Lawrence. His research interests include the portrayal of health information in the mass media and new communication technologies, the moderation of effects of qualitative and quantitative evidence types on health-related decision making, the effects of new technologies on organizations, and the rhetoric of science. He has published in *Advancing the Consumer Interest* and was the recipient of the 1999 Bruce Kendall Award for Excellence in Teaching at Purdue University.